# WADDLE

# WADDLE

## The authorised biography of Chris Waddle

by
MEL STEIN

COCKEREL BOOKS LTD

Published by Cockerel Books Ltd
23-25 Maddox Street
London W1R 9LE

Photoset in North Wales by
Derek Doyle & Associates, Mold, Clwyd
Printed in Great Britain by
Butler & Tanner Ltd
Somerset

# Introduction

It is with great pleasure and satisfaction that I write the Introduction to this book which, without doubt, is an inspiration to all young boys who want to be successful football players. This is a story of rejection; of being employed in other jobs apart from football; of working hard at football when given another chance to succeed; and of the ups and downs, the highs and lows of Professional Football.

My own involvement with Chris started at Newcastle United in September 1980. He had just joined the Club from Tow Law Football Club as a 19-year-old who had been to Coventry City and Sunderland for trials, but who was allowed to leave. Now he was being given another chance to succeed. For a big lad he was very skillful, he had two excellent feet, but also unmistakable running style which gave the impression that he was always tired. He was very quiet and appeared to lack confidence until he got the football to his feet.

I am not in the least surprised at the success Chris has had and I now feel fully justified in treating him the way I did in his early years at St James' Park. I think there were days, and even weeks, when he perhaps considered not coming to work – but he had everything a football player needed to be a success and it was a matter of making him realise that fact! I think he has done so, to the benefit of Newcastle, Tottenham, England and, most of all, himself.

I wish him continued success on the football fields of the world and in whatever other interests he may pursue after football. I feel this book is a stimulus to all young boys, clearly carrying as it does the motto 'if at first you don't succeed then try try again'. Chris did just that and he has been well and truly rewarded, both mentally and physically.

Arthur Cox
Manager, Derby County FC
August 1988

# Acknowledgements

To Newcastle United and
all the young Geordies
whose stories have yet to
be written.

Mel Stein

To Lorna and Brooke
And thanks to many
people, including my
family; all the friends I've
not had space to mention
here – in particular those
from The Kingfisher, who
made us feel so at home so
quickly; Jim Pearson of
Nike, who offered me my
first contract and then
stuck with it; and all the
players I've had the pleasure to play with.

Chris Waddle

# Prologue

*I couldn't believe it. Standing in the dole queue waiting to be called forward. It was unreal. If you work you get paid, that was what my parents had always taught me, and football was the only work I knew. Yet here I was, having signed on with Coventry as a schoolboy and then been dropped, about to be paid for doing nought.*

*I have always hated losing and have never regarded myself as a loser, but that day I surely felt like one. It wasn't my fault I was without a job, any more than it's the fault of most people; but fault or not it didn't help. Christopher Waddle, superstar on the rubbish heap at sixteen years of age. If people think I hunch my shoulders now they should have seen me that day, trying to make myself look smaller, trying to make myself invisible.*

*The clerk took forever writing down my details, stamping the forms, shuffling pieces of paper and getting my signature a dozen times. It was a signature then, it's an autograph now. If you'd asked me that day whether I'd play for England and travel the world, whether I'd have kids lining up for that autograph, I'd have laughed in your face. Or cried.*

*Finally I held the cheque in my hand —£10.30. That was all I had in the world; that and my two legs; that and a burning ambition to show them all that they were wrong. Coventry City, I thought, one day I'll be back and then you'll be sorry. In one way my short and not-so-sweet career had just finished, in another, it had just begun …*

# CHAPTER 1

Leam Lane, Gateshead sounds as unromantic as it looks. Today children still play in its grey streets, kicking their footballs wearing either the red and white of Sunderland or Newcastle's famous black and white stripes, their rivalry every bit as fierce and competitive as that of their real life heroes. In eighteen years very little has changed. The houses are a little older, a little more begrimed by the coal dust that seems to drift in from nowhere and settle everywhere; but the heroes are different. Sunderland languish in the lower reaches of the League, Billy Hughes is gone; Vic Halom long since retired; John McGrath, Newcastle's iron man, has turned his gentle talents to management and Jim Iley's balding midfield skills are a distant memory of art and craft amidst blood and brawn.

Joseph Waddle's memories of Sunderland went back far further than the 1960's. He'd supported them almost since his birth in 1914 and in his childhood had nurtured the dream that one day he would pull on a red and white striped shirt and would score a winning goal, to turn and bask in the adulation of the Roker Roar. The reality was, as usual, a million light years away from the dreams.

Joe Waddle left school in 1928 at fourteen and followed the family tradition by going down the pits at that tender age; not for him the wide open spaces of Roker Park, not for him the sharing of a dressing room with Len Shackleton. His days were spent in the twilight zone beneath the ground where the coal dust that he gulped down instead of air was to damage his health for ever. There was to be no luxuriating in a warm bath after the match, but rather the shared cold water that made little or no impression on the blackness that became engrained into every pore of his skin and bit not a little deeply into his soul.

Joe had every reason to hope that professional football would rescue him from the mine. Two footed, unlike the boy who was to

9

be his youngest son and succeed where he had failed, he was able to play at either inside left or inside right and appeared regularly as an amateur for Pelaw. He and his six brothers lived and breathed football. If each day he died a little death underground then football was his oxygen, his life-blood received its regular transfusions by playing every evening after school and work. Then in 1939 when Joe was twenty-five a madman with a small moustache in Germany shattered his dreams. Joe joined the Navy and sailed away from Weirside for the duration of the war, and from professional football for ever.

Elizabeth Ashton had a less traditional background. Her mother came from Ashton, near Wigan and she came south in the war to join her numerous sisters who lived in Watford. She met and married Joe and with his two brothers and four sisters and Elizabeth's sisters it was a perfect opportunity for the British Film Industry to make its own version of *Seven Brides for Seven Brothers*, an opportunity which needless to say they spurned.

After their marriage Elizabeth and Joseph settled down in Gateshead. Elizabeth worked first in the Physiotherapy Department of a local hospital and then for the local Co-operative. Joe meanwhile had surfaced and was now employed by the Monckton Coke Works. Coal would come out of the pit, be brought to the works and then burned and transformed into coke by Joseph Waddle and his workmates. Wherever you were in those post war years in the North-East you could be sure that somehow or other the great God of coal had a part to play in your destiny.

In 1955 Joe and Elizabeth had their first son, Raymond, followed three years later by Joseph Junior. With their two sons Joe felt that his footballing dynasty was assured. Further inspired by his many sisters-in-law he and Elizabeth decided to embark upon parenthood once more, on the basis that they felt sure a combination of instinct and fate would guarantee them a daughter. Throughout Elizabeth's pregnancy the growing child was referred to as 'her', even to the extent of choice of names. December 1960 arrived; Elvis Presley's *It's Now or Never* entered its sixth week at No 1 in the pop music charts; John Kennedy was into his first month as the youngest ever US President; Pope John the 23rd and the Archbishop of Canterbury Dr Fisher came face to face in the first Anglican-Catholic meeting since the two religions split in 1543; cinemagoers were watching *Exodus* and *The Alamo* ... and then on 14 December the third child of the union of Joe and Elizabeth Waddle was born. The selected name of Gail had to be immediately abandoned and Christopher Roland had arrived. Even if Joe did not have his daughter he at least had his midfield trio!

By the time Christopher was three, in 1963, the family were on the move again – to another council house this time at 29 Gosforth Terrace, Pelaw. Ray by now was attending Roman Road school, which was soon to have another new pupil in the shape of Lorna Bruce, whose family were also from Leam Lane. Years later that same little girl became Lorna Waddle.

The whole Waddle family was football crazy; Joseph supported Sunderland, as did Ray, while Joe Junior divided his loyalties between Sunderland and another team to have made a tradition out of red and white – Arsenal. Elizabeth was not the sort of woman to bide at home whilst her menfolk were standing on the terraces. When Joseph was unable to take the boys to Roker Park, Elizabeth would shepherd her three sons there with pride and stand alongside them no less fervent than they. Len Shackleton, the Clown Prince of Soccer, was her special hero and when she watched her youngest son practising with a ball it was always 'Len wouldn't do it like that,' or 'Len would have tried this.'

The talent scouts were out watching Christopher at a very young age. His father was not averse to a day out at the races and invariably wherever the Waddle Clan went a ball was likely to accompany them. It was in 1963 at Wetherby races when a friend of Joe's stood and watched the diminutive Chris kicking a ball against the wall. Time and time again the child controlled the ball with his left foot, hammered it back, controlled it again, then repeated the process with unerring accuracy. 'That lad'll be a professional one day,' the friend said. His father with a knowing smile of pride did not disagree.

At the back of the Waddle house were five playing fields. One was earmarked for a local Catholic school, the others for pubs and clubs. Christopher would see his older brothers off to school and then fret the rest of the day away awaiting their return. From three in the afternoon he would take up his post in the bay window looking down Gosforth Terrace for the first sight of the school uniform that meant he had somebody with whom to play football. It didn't really matter what he wore in those days, Ray and Joe Junior's hand-me-downs were perfectly acceptable – all he wanted was to be allowed to join in with the two older brothers he idolised in much the same way that they in turn worshipped the Sunderland first team.

# WADDLE

In one way at least Chris couldn't wait to get to school. There'd be other boys there, other lads as football-daft as he was himself, and other bodies meant a team, a real team. By the time he started at Bill Quay Junior Mixed Infants in 1965 Ray had already made the school team and eventually moved on to be selected for Jarrow, Hepburn and Feltham. Joe Junior, without quite the talents of his older brother, also made the school team and it just remained for Chris to establish a record for the Waddles, who were the first three brothers all to play for the Bill Quay side.

Bill Quay Mixed Infants did not have the luxury of a specialist Sports Master. That role was filled by an elderly English teacher, Mr Martin. Young Joe was always a big fan of the even younger Chris. He led his kid brother over to Mr Martin. 'Can our kid have a trial for the team?' he asked. Mr Martin looked down at the tot. 'How old is he?' 'Six,' replied Joe, deciding there was little or no point in lying about his brother's age. Mr Martin shrugged. He knew all about the persistence of the older Waddles. 'He can have a go,' he replied.Chris did more than have a go. At six years old he seized the first opportunity that was offered to him and made the team along with kids three or four years older and twice his size. The Chris Waddle football career was on the move.

# CHAPTER 2

Chris Waddle never set Bill Quay Mixed Infants School alight in academic terms. Whilst Ray was above average and Joe really bright, for Chris lessons were really an extended break between sports. As he grew it was painfully obvious that sport was the only thing he was ever going to be really good at. It wasn't that he was stupid, it was just that he found it virtually impossible to concentrate on anything that did not involve a football. Somehow, even at that early age, within himself he had the supreme confidence that his sporting skill would always earn him a living.

The school did not have the resources to buy a strip specially to fit the tiny Chris. His shirt was so long that it came straight through his shorts and down to his knees. Very little about that team was serious. Joe Waddle was the goal keeper, with Chris up front and the team was beaten very regularly by margins of as much as eight or nine goals. Joe's goalkeeping was to say the least erratic. In one match against Haworth, a rival school with a bit of a reputation for demolition of weak opposion, Joe demonstrated his usual lack of concentration with regard to keeping the ball out from between the posts. Throughout the match he insisted on leaning against one of the uprights talking to a friend. Haworth were not unmindful of the situation and shot from great distances at every opportunity. By the time a Bill Quay team member had shouted a warning to Joe there was little for him to do but pick the ball out of the net, boot it down field and then resume his conversation.

The 1966 World Cup had set the fashion for overhead kicks, but unfortunately for Bill Quay Joe was no Brazilian. His first effort to kick the ball away while facing his own goal resulted in the ball going straight up in the air, giving the opposing centre-forward the easiest chance to tap the ball home. Mr Martin's patience was exhausted and Joe was moved from goal to right-back. On his debut in that position the ball flew towards him in the first five minutes. Realising it was going over his head he grew wings and

13

caught the ball spectacularly, completely forgetting his enforced resignation from his goalkeeper's role. Mr Martin, surprised by little that Joe Waddle did, quietly cautioned him. A few minutes later a pass was going down his righthand side. Joe threw himself in that direction and palmed the ball away for a throw in.

It did not really need a crystal ball to see that Joe Waddle's future was not to be on the football field. As it was, it would be a long time before his future was finally decided. Easily led at school he got in with the wrong crowd at the comprehensive he attended and left at fifteen without ever fulfilling his academic potential. Joe Junior always followed the trends, first a skinhead, then into heavy metal. He began working in an office at Lumsdens, met his wife there and then moved on to another mundane office job at Timex. It was only when he became unemployed on that company's liquidation that he finally decided to concentrate on his life and he is now studying at Teacher Training College, before launching himself on the unspecting world of contemporary Joe Waddles.

As it was, in the 1960's Joe drifted away from the companionship of his two younger brothers and would seek his sanctuary on the streets, roaming and smoking with a group of friends that Mrs Waddle found less than desirable. As Joe Junior grew even further apart from both his brothers and Chris in particular, the youngest Waddle latched on to Ray like a limpet. Over the next few years Ray became much more than an older brother, he became an extention of Chris' own being. The familiar sound in the Waddle household was, 'where's Ray?' or 'when's Ray coming in?' Wherever Ray Waddle went, the smaller Chris was never very far behind.

At this time Joe's hopes for a professional footballing son rested with Ray. He would follow his son all over the North-East to watch him play, but although he attracted scouts from the likes of Burnley no firm offer was ever made. Then at around the age of twelve Ray's talent suddenly seemed to freeze. Other kids got bigger and stronger and more skilful and gradually it became apparent that another Waddle son was about to disappoint his father in sporting terms. Ray was not as heartbroken as his father about his limitation. He was always a very friendly boy, able to overcome every obstacle adversity put in his way. He was happy just to play football with his friends, games that Chris was always allowed to join. Not for Ray the streets or the discos. There was just football, football, football until the last dregs of daylight had been drained dry and it was time to watch *Match of the Day*. Never that keen on school he joined his mother in the Co-op at fifteen making pots and pans, then worked as a van boy for a tea company. Finally he joined a local bus company as a conductor, graduated to driving and today still thoroughly enjoys his lot, happy for himself and his family and particularly happy over the career of Chris.

The whole of the Waddle family was happy in the summer of 1967. The memory of England's triumph in the World Cup just twelve months earlier was still fresh in their minds. It is amazing what an impact such an event had upon the ordinary working class Englishman. The Israelis might be recapturing Jerusalem in the Middle East but for the Waddles and millions like them the summer of 1967 was still that golden time when British football was on top of the world. The family headed for Butlin's Holiday Camp at Ayr that year. The days were spent playing snooker, table tennis or the inevitable football, whilst in the evenings even the youngest of the Waddle boys would join his brothers in the camp disco, singing along to the Beatles and the Monkees.

*All You Need Is Love* sang the Beatles that summer, and Chris certainly had his fair share of that from his family. Although the money was hardly flowing into the household coffers Joe and Elizabeth always made sure that the boys had everything they needed – even if they had to do without themselves. As far as the boys were concerned what they thought they most needed were football boots. In 1967 Stylo Boots, favoured by George Best, were all the rage and the boys would adapt Power Point stickers to affix to them. These took the form of coloured numbers – for example a number four would be stuck on the back of the heel and as Chris flicked the ball backwards he'd shout excitedly: 'I've done a four!' So intense was the belief in the magic of Georgie Best that Chris would buy no other bubble gum than that endorsed by the Belfast Boy, convinced that merely chewing it would ensure that he became a better player.

Shortly after they returned from their holiday in Scotland Joe Senior took his sons to what was Chris' first match. Inevitably it was at Roker Park; Sunderland were playing Middlesborough in a Youth Cup tie. The three boys were actually taken into the stands to sit and watch the game, the height of luxury in those days. Unfortunately Sunderland lost 2-1.

The seven-year-old Chris was remarkably quiet at school, sometimes going a whole day without saying a single word in class. He was (and still is to some extent) painfully shy until he got to know anybody and Elizabeth would have to escort him daily.

# WADDLE

When it was time to go home, however, he was, in his own words, 'like Ben Johnson out of his blocks.' The days took on a routine of their own; his mother would take him to school, he'd daydream away the day, often playing coin football on his desk top, then he would race home to play real football with his brother Ray and his friends.

It was his geography teacher who summed it up in one report; 'if his brains were in his feet he'd win *Mastermind*.' Little did that teacher know that those feet were to win far greater prizes than any on offer in the final of a television quiz programme.

# CHAPTER 3

Bill Quay Junior Mixed Infants was not the Blackboard Jungle but then it wasn't Eton either. Chris' best friend at school was Peter Allen who lived along the road from Chris in Pelaw. Peter was a well-built strong lad of average height, a goalkeeper by ambition who would be railroaded into practice sessions by Chris who would hit the ball at him until his hands were painful. Peter and Chris were to play together in every team until Chris joined Tow Law. The boys were never in the same class at school but Peter was never slow to encourage Chris in the playground. Chris was not a violent lad yet somehow or other he got the reputation of being the best fighter in the school. Looking back now he realises that this was based upon one fight and one fight alone. There was a particular boy whom everybody steered clear of, capable as he was of demolishing boys years older than himself. Eventually, with some encouragement from Peter and Chris' other 'friends', a match was made between Chris and the school champion, a fight that attracted nearly as much attention as the Bruno-Bugner battle Chris and thousands of others recently watched at White Hart Lane. The two boys fought for what seemed like hours until each decided that their pride was intact with a draw. After that, even at Senior School, Chris never had to fight.

On the football field he had no need to draw blood. In his second-last year in the Juniors the school team, in their claret and blue strip, got to the Charity Shield Final. This was played at Hawthorn Lesley's ground, the local schoolboys' Wembley. The opposition was St Matthews. Neither team was able to break the deadlock until Chris latched on to a long ball. He ran from the half-way line, the keeper came out, Chris swerved around him and not for the last time in his life hammered the ball into the roof of the net. One-nil to Bill Quay and Chris had the taste of winning.

At that time (and even today, some critics might say) his talents were limited to his ability to dribble. His frail frame gave no real opportunity for the physical side of the game and he was a ready target for intimidation. He remembers one match against Linney House, which harboured some of the toughest kids in the district. A lad nick-named 'Whitey' was right-back. Chris' reputation preceded him and Linney House (and Whitey in particular) had got the message that if you stopped Waddle you went a long way to stopping the team. Within ten minutes one violent kick from Whitey had actually broken Chris' shin pad. Thereafter every time Chris got the ball that round object was incidental to Whitey's aim. Despite the treatment being meted out to him, or perhaps because of it, Chris then scored. Scared to hold on to the ball for more than five seconds he hit a long shot which bounced over the Linney House 'keeper and into the net. Chris took one look at Whitey and couldn't decide whether to celebrate or write his will. As he had nothing to leave in those days, he decided discretion was the better part of valour and retreated to centre-half where he played out the rest of the match away from Whitey's gentle attentions. Curiously enough the two boys were to become firm friends at their secondary school.

That school team of Chris' went from strength to strength and came through thirty-three teams to be Runners-up in the Heburn League. Yet football was not the only sport at which Chris excelled. An annual local event was the Fellamy Fair at Haworth Cricket Ground for the under elevens. Chris was chosen with three others to run the relay. Linney House were again hot favourites and were coasting home with St Augustus second. The St Augustus runner lifted the baton as he ran on into the straight, 'yes, we got second!' he shouted triumphantly; but he'd not taken into account the determination of Chris Waddle running the last leg for Bill Quay. Pursuing the other boy even when all seemed lost he caught him on the line to take his first medal home. Even then he did not take to losing easily. In that same year he won his school's cross country which was twice around the sports field. His liking for long distance running evaporated when he was fourteen, however, and now the sheer boredom of it is anathema to him.

His speed and staying power as a child did his football career no harm at all. He moved easily up the school and indeed had a trial for the area district team when he was only six years and ten months. The rest of the team were ten years old. As he progressed through the school years so the team also improved. In his final year at Bill Quay no adult was prepared to take the side. Mr Smith had left. Chris came home desolate, faced with the prospect of the team disbanding. Joseph Waddle Senior could not stand the thought of yet another of his sons drifting away from the game and took over as the manager, unofficial, unpaid and ultimately unappreciated. He took the team to the top of the League, scrambling for glory with Town Avenue, for whom another of the North-East's favourite sons was to pull on a shirt, a young man who was to achieve glory not on the football field but on the running track – Steve Cram.

When Bill Quay were at their peak a teacher decided that the glory should be kept in-house and wanted to take over the side. It was hard to tell who was the more disconsolate – father or son. It was the son who made up his mind to do something about it. He stormed in to see his Headmaster.

'You can't replace my dad.'

'We can't?' There was an icy note in the Headmaster's voice.

'If my dad's not manager, then I don't play.'

'All right, don't play.'

The Headmaster regarded the interview at an end. Chris was astonished. He knew that he was the best player in the team, but then false modesty has never been part of his make-up. It was his first real clash with authority, his first intimation that football does not just exist on the field, that there are politics which transcend the game itself and which ultimately create a division between directors and management, and management and players.

As it was, for reasons probably unconnected with his son's stand, Joe Waddle kept the job. The team battled on wearing a kit of green with amber sleeves and green and amber socks. Chris and two other boys chose it from a catalogue and as he says now it was truly 'disgusting.'

Chris' life was filled with football that last year at Bill Quay Juniors. He was by now the lynchpin of the Jarrow Hepburn and Feltham District team who went out of the District Cup to Durham Boys, losing by a single goal in a raging gale. Durham Boys went on to win the cup 8-1 so that was no disgrace.

Playing alongside Chris for the District Team was his inseperable friend Peter Allen. Pete had moved out of goal to left-back for the school team and his father had become Joe Waddle's quasi-assistant in the management of the side. The season ended in disappointment for the team. They won nothing, being pipped by Town Avenue for the League; yet for Chris the season was a personal triumph. He scored 66 goals, failing to find the net in only one match. It was the end of Joe Waddle's managerial career and for Chris it was goodbye to Bill Quay.

# CHAPTER 4

For a footballer of the eighties to have neither telephone nor car is unheard of; but in the sixties and early seventies they were still the ultimate luxury for many a North-Eastern family. Joe Waddle had driven his family around on a motorbike and sidecar since Chris was very small. The Waddles presented an interesting sight as Joe would put on his helmet and goggles, Elizabeth would sit behind him and the three boys would cram into the sidecar for the seven hour trip down South to see their relations in Watford. Elizabeth would cling desperately to her husband as the boys would invent a guessing game that approximated to Russian Roulette on wheels. In these pre-motorway days it was still possible to drive at speeds of up to 60 mph and the terrible trio would jump around between the second and third seats of the sidecar with cheerful cries to their trembling mother: 'Hey Mam, guess which one of us is in the back seat now?'

Joe Senior had always collected sixpences and eventually, when Chris was nearly ten, he staggered along to his local garage with a huge plastic bag containing £50 worth of the now defunct coin. For that precise sum he purchased his first car and proudly drove it back home and even more proudly took the family for a drive around the town. The Waddles had a car, the Waddles in Geordie terms had arrived. Unfortunately for all concerned Joseph had forgotten one thing; he'd not passed his driving test and indeed he never did. The car seemed to understand and accept the position better than the rest of the family, for after that first illegal trip it never went again. He was soon back to the motorbike. When he decided to sell that the purchaser also decided he'd like thrown in for free the toolkit that Joe had meticulously collected and cared for over the years, that was taken without Joe's consent and Joe never saw the purchaser, the bike or the toolkit again. After that it was back to the push-bike.

At the same time that Chris left Bill Quay Junior School the family moved to 1 Kier Hardie Avenue, Wardley. Joe Senior was delighted by the address. He was a lifetime Labour supporter who had no time for private enterprise. He firmly believed in the nationalisation of everything, although nobody can remember as to whether or not that included professional football. Chris can, however, clearly recall him shouting at Edward Heath when he appeared on television, and moaning throughout *Top of the Pops*, a programme he could hardly have expected his youngest son to appear upon with not one, but two, top twenty hits.

His father was still working at Monckton Coke Works at the time of the move. There at the coke ovens he would take the coal, the North-East's own precious metal, cut it down to size, pour water on it to transform it into coke. A hard job for a tough man. Friday was wages day and during his holidays Chris would accompany his father to collect his wage packet, riding the red chopper that his adored brother Ray had bought him. It had cost £32 and had taken Ray weeks of saving. For the Waddles in those days the family was everything, or at least nearly everything, for friends meant something too.

The move to Kier Hardie Avenue had taken them into the heart of Chris' friends. At No 6 lived Keith Mullen also a life-long Sunderland supporter. Keith was red and white mad, distracted only by his obsession with David Bowie. Keith, without a red and white scarf or a Bowie 'T' shirt, was later to be Chris' best man. Around the corner in Kirkwood Gardens lived the Renicks, Keith, Brian and Colin, a charismatic trio with whom everyone wanted to play. Then in the same road, last but by no means least lived Chris' best friend the unique Gary Durham.

Bill Quay Junior School had previously spilled out its unacademic children to Highfields but that had become too full so Chris and Gary went to Hewarth Grange. Elizabeth Waddle formed an immediate and lasting dislike of little Gary Durham. Chris, however, would delight in going to school with him. The boys should have been there at nine for assembly but Chris was not a great fan of assemblies. Neither he nor any of his family ever went to Church, not even at Christmas, for much the same reason – they simply did not like being preached at. Even today Chris favours managers who are short and sharp to the point. He has a very low boredom threshold and believes if you can say in five words something that could take twenty then five will do.

Assemblies at Hewarth Grange, which consisted of hymn singing and a general talk, were not high on Chris' required viewing list.

# WADDLE

He and Gary would deliberately get there at 9.30 in time for registration but with yet another time-wasting ace up their schoolboy sleeves. Any pupil arriving without a tie would be sent home automatically to fetch it. Chris would go into school about twenty yards ahead of Gary, tie in his pocket, and promptly be sent home. Gary would follow and meet the same fate. Together they'd amble away for half an hour or so and would return with their ties around their necks and a mumbled apology that they didn't have a key and had to find their mothers.

Gary Durham was always bright and inventive, a sort of Bilko of his generation. In one year he started in the top group while Chris was in the bottom group. To be with his friend Gary simply did no work and got himself relegated. Mrs Waddle blamed Gary for everything, but in fact it was probably Gary's friendship with Chris which halted Gary's academic progress. Gary is now a butcher with ambitions to enter the police force and there is little doubt that if he makes it Gary Durham may well be the John Stalker of the 21st century …

Chris' football career was flourishing even if he was not spending a full day at school. He made the under twelve team straight away, a good side with enormous potential. His old friend Peter Allen was in goal, there was John Tweedie, who Chris thought might have made it professionally but who ended up at Gateshead, and Steven Higgins who joined Tweedie at the same club, Stephen Webb who was to play alongside Chris at Tow Law, and Paul Curtiss who played in the Northern League. The team had its characters as well as its skilful players – there was Barry Charlton, he and Chris became very friendly, who stood 5' 9' in his stockinged feet at eleven years of age, and Ian Kennedy the school bully who eventually grew to like Chris because he made goals for him.

In the early days Kennedy didn't like Chris quite enough not to demand his dinner money with menaces. Chris would say he hadn't got it, having taken it out of his pocket and put it in his hand when he'd seen the boy coming. Whitey – the same Whitey who'd broken Chris's shin pad, was Kennedy's side kick and would frisk Chris gangster-fashion at a nod from his boss. They never found anything and it never occured to Whitey to get Chris to open his hand. It was also noted with interest that he and Kennedy would never play in away games with the team. Because he was the school bully his reputation preceded him and the opposition school bully would be waiting for him. Strength did not necessarily mean bravery. Chris might not have been learning about maths and geography, but he was learning in the school of life, every day and in every way.

# CHAPTER 5

By the time Chris was thirteen a whole host of professional clubs were watching him. The school team was playing in the full Durham League and after one particular match, when they beat St Aidens of Sunderland 5-4 with Chris scoring two and making two, Joseph Waddle was approached by Sheffied United, Blackpool and Leeds. Joe had actually attended that match with a cine camera and had caught three of the goals for posterity. Also immortalised on film is the kit combination of a yellow shirt with two blue hoops backed by a big white patch with a red number, blue shorts and yellow socks. The team looked more like exotic birds than footballers. Nevertheless, Chris' talent shone through as he made his way to goal wearing the Adidas boots that his dad always bought for him, as a tribute to the skill of Franz Beckenbauer who endorsed them in those days.

It wasn't just at home that Chris was receiving encouragement of his talent. In his first year at school there were three PE teachers – a Mr Buxton who left and went off to Liverpool, doubtless to teach kids who'd grace Anfield and Goodison, a Mr Davison, who never warmed to Chris, and Mr Fawcett who finally ended up taking the team. Mr Fawcett had a good sense of humour which touched a familiar spot in Chris and his fellow team members. He'd had a bad knee injury in the past, but still had a nice delicate touch. He'd a fine team with which to work and they responded to the man. He was enthusiastic and it rubbed off, and his excitement at managing a winning team could not have been exceeded by any League manager whose team did the double.

Yet if his football career was taking off Chris was becoming totally lost in the academic backwaters. French was anathema to him as he could never understand why he should want to speak it. That question now addressed to close friends Glen Hoddle and Mark Hateley might bring an interesting response. There were also some brutal teachers at the school who had little or no time for the shy, dreaming Chris. One in particular would shake him violently and say loudly enough for everyone to hear, 'are you in love Waddle?' Chris would just sit, tremble and blush, a nervous boy who needed a sensitive approach to bring out the best in him. That same man wrote to Chris recently telling him he was teaching in London and would Chris like to meet him. Chris tore up the letter. He is not a person to hate or bear grudges but he cannot stand hypocrisy.

He quite enjoyed history and geography, but even worse than French was woodwork. The woodwork teacher, a Mr Sanderson, did not take prisoners. His main exchanges of conversation with Chris were 'blithering dolt' every time Chris forgot to bring something into the lesson. Needless to say Chris didn't shine at the subject. He'd shake and lie awake the night before the lesson and was the only boy in the school never to finish any project in three years – he particularly remembers one little bookcase with sliding rails which he thought he'd completed only to receive three out of ten.

His school career came to a climax at the end of his third year at Hewarth Grange. There was a choice of subjects but the Chemistry teacher made it quite plain that he did not want Chris Waddle in his class. The Physics teacher jumped on the anti-Waddle bandwagon which really began to gather momentum when the Biology teacher stated that Waddle did not figure in his first team selection. The choices beyond that were limited to say the least. He was left with Physical Education and Community Service to which were added the compulsory subjects of Maths, English and Foreign Studies. The Headmaster invited Chris to see him and told him in no uncertain terms that the combination of subjects that he thought Chris had chosen – but which in fact had been imposed on him – was unheard of, unworkable and totally unacceptable. Chris argued his innocence in vain and was sent back to the teachers with a message from the Headmaster that they should reconsider their decisions. This they duly did and their answer was still no, so Chris set out on the dubious road that led to Community Service.

Community Service involved going out to old people's homes to do jobs that probably didn't need doing and which even if they did the elderly did not want done by a bored fourteen year old schoolboy. It got to the stage by the end of the first week that on Friday afternoon Chris simply gave up and went home to watch television, a pastime that has always rated highly on his list of leisure activities.

Thereafter hedge cutting and lawn mowing were largely ignored, with his mother joining in the innocent deception by signing the work book in different names to confirm satisfaction with the undone jobs. The school never enquired further and honour was duly satisfied on both sides. As far as Foreign Studies were concerned, to this day Chris has never found out what it was all about and after a couple of weeks of total bemusement he eventually gave up.

At that stage in his life there was no intimation of a musical career and he was not even part of the school choir. All he lived for was football. Come the weekend his parents, along with most of their close-knit community would go off to the Social Clubs. Chris would play football on a Saturday morning and then go to watch Sunderland play in the afternoon under the management of Allan Brown, a much respected man in the North-East. After the match there was more kicking a ball around the streets or maybe the sophistication of such street games as knocking on doors and running away. Sundays were also geared to football, playing with his friends, then watching *The Big Match* on television, then out again. 'I'm George Best,' 'I'm Denis Law,' 'I'm Bobby Charlton.' It was the age of the hero, the age of adulation, an age when eleven nonentities could achieve success by kicking balls high and far in the air and kicking the opposition even further.

Gary Durham, Peter Allen, and the Renicks all supported Newcastle, whilst Chris and Keith Mullen still stayed loyal to Sunderland. From that team Chris was impressed by Billy Hughes, a totally left sided player; Jimmy Montgomery the talented goalkeeper who'd brought the Cup to Weirside with his miraculous double save; and George Hird who'd do a cartwheel if he scored a goal and would entertain the crowds by balancing a ball on the back of his neck. When Chris finally joined Newcastle George was in charge of the youth team.

The world may be small but the footballing world is even smaller. For example, in January 1988 Chris was sitting at Barnet with the writer watching them play Windsor at an FA Trophy replay. He suddenly recognised the Windsor full-back as having played with him in schoolboy matches in the North-East. Yes, a really small world and one in which there is very little room for the outsider. When friends and family go into the Players' Lounge for drinks after the match, when directors go into the dressing room, they are never really a part of that world, they are the intruders. When a player retires or is invalided out of the game it makes it just that much harder to join the real world outside, the real world where people have studied chemistry, physics, biology and French, the real world where yesterday's heroes are today's forgotten men.

# CHAPTER 6

People talk about the sixties with affection but to the teenage Chris Waddle the seventies were no less gentle a time. Sunderland triumphed at Wembley in 1973, 1974 was the year of Slade, of Mud, of Abba, Gary Glitter, David Essex, the Osmonds, the Three Degrees; a year which began with President Nixon refusing to comply with a Court Order demanding delivery of the 'White House Tapes', a year of unrest in Chris' native North-East when a three day working week to save electricity was followed by a go-slow by miners and railworkers in the United Kingdom. These were not matters of great concern to Chris. He was more interested in the effect on football, the fact that clubs could not play floodlit matches unless they had their own generators, the fact that there was a new tide rising in the North-East as Newcastle under Joe Harvey, following Sunderland's success; began a run that was to lead to their destruction at Wembley in May by Liverpool. If 1973 was Sunderland's year, 1974 was no time to be a Sunderland supporter, at least not until after Keegan and Heighway had knocked those three nails in United's coffin.

It was a time of remarkable innocence. Chris and his friends would play catching kissing in the streets – Alison Monroe was the first girl he recalls having a crush on, a year younger than him she lived five minutes away if you ran, and kids ran everywhere in those days – there seemed to be so much to do and so little time. Chris and the boys (and the girls) would spend the evenings sitting outside their houses on the low walls just talking and smoking. Chris never smoked although everybody else seemed to and everybody thought he did because he never refused a cigarette. 'I've just had one – I'll save it till later,' he'd say then give his haul to the incorrigible Gary Durham.

Chris can never remember not wanting to be a professional footballer, he never toyed with the typical childish romance of driving an engine or walking on the moon, for him a grass field was

28

good enough – these were the days, it must be remembered when, as his current manager once wrote, *They Used to Play on Grass*. His father was happy to let him get on with whatever he wanted to do whilst his mother, despite her complicity in his community service scam, was always urging him to study. However, her urging had very little effect because in five years at secondary school he can only remember doing about half a dozen bits of homework. Usually, to avoid dire repercussions at school, he'd get his brother Joe to help him – for a small fee.

Elizabeth Waddle was beginning to despair of Joe. He had a brain but simply wouldn't apply himself. He'd be in and out of the house, eat, then off with his less than desirable mates, chatting up girls and smoking. On one occasion Elizabeth found him smoking and immediately went out and bought him a long thick cigar which she lit up for him then and there hoping to teach him a lesson once and for all. Joe manfully worked his way through it in front of Chris and his mother getting greener and greener then finally wreathed in smoke said, 'have you got any more for later, Mam.'

Joe was the innovator in the family, the rebel, the first to smoke, to drink, to get a motorbike. Yet it was the quiet Ray who married first. Chris can only recall his brother ever having two girlfriends before he met his wife to be, Carol. One was a girl from Birmingham he met in Butlins and, very much encouraged, the sixteen-year-old Ray went down to the Midlands himself on the train – only to be greeted by the girl and a young man whom she cheerfully introduced as her boyfriend!

Really the Waddle family in the early 1970's were no different from a hundred other families on Tyneside or Weirside. Most of them would go to Butlins for their holidays, for most a colour TV and a car were the limits of their ambitions and with that ambition achieved they were satisfied with their lot. It was the only world Chris knew, a life of security and routine, a safe life where anything unusual shone out like a beacon. He recalls Joe taking him to see Status Quo at Newcastle City Hall when he was thirteen. Joe was always one for odd clothes and wore a cassock that night. A pigeon decided to relieve itself right on it and Joe immediately looked up and said with a wry grin, 'Ee, I thought I was on your side tonight.'

It is that gentle humour, the warmth and generosity of his family that permeates Chris' childhood and teens, a generosity reflected in his mother buying him ten different football strips, including Sunderland (home and away), Wolves, Rangers, (he declined Celtic), West Ham, QPR. QPR was his favourite probably because

29

he was so impressed by the mercurial skills of Rodney Marsh. Gary Durham inevitably had a part to play in the history of Chris Waddle's football kit. He once loaned Gary his Sunderland away kit. Gary was incredibly lackadaisical and just left it in Chris's unlocked locker from which it was not surprisingly stolen overnight. He was terrified to tell his mother and even more terrified to mention Gary Durham's name. He took the blame himself and received a verbal onslaught rather than the instant death that would have accompanied Gary's involvement.

At that time it was what the strip looked like that attracted Chris, not who the teams were – the old gold of Wolves, West Ham away with its light blue and two claret hoops, but however many kits Elizabeth bought him he never owned an England or a Tottenham Hotspur shirt – they were still a million miles away.

# CHAPTER 7

Although other clubs had been watching and enquiring, the first positive steps to attract Chris' signature as soon as he was old enough came from Newcastle, with Coventry, Blackpool and Leeds not far behind.

Newcastle had gone through the ritual of watching him a few times then went ahead with the age-old scenario of coming to his house and telling his parents that he was the best thing since sliced bread. A conversation and scenario repeated daily by scouts up and down the country. Chris was then only thirteen and was therefore unable to sign even schoolboy forms until he was fourteen in December 1974. Through Les Cummins and Tommy Jordan, the scouts (a great double act sadly separated when Tommy died a few years later), Chris trained twice a week at St James' Park. This training was taken by Geoff Allen.

At first it seemed like a dream. He'd be picked up in a car and taken to the ground. They'd arrive there at five-thirty, would be changed for six and there the dream ended because they'd have to walk a mile up the road in their boots and shirts, even on the coldest of nights. There was no luxury of a track suit for the boys and certainly no minibus to take them there and back. Indeed, those who supervised their training had the gall to complain that the metal was showing through the studs ignoring the fact that they had been worn down by the long walk to the training ground. The dream was shattered completely when Peter Allen, who'd accompanied Chris, was dropped. The boys had played together in every team but their paths were about to separate temporarily in footballing terms. Obviously Newcastle thought they had their lad and lost interest. Chris had to get to the ground by bus to the City Centre and then on foot. He'd do one-and-a-half hours there, collect his expenses and then it was the long trek back home in the dark without any concern being shown by the club for his safety.

The training itself was often disjointed and unsatisfactorily

31

organised giving more the feeling of a boys' club than a footballing outfit. Not even the same person was in charge each week. Once Keith Burkinshaw took possession, then Geoff Allen and Chris, even at the tender age of thirteen, decided he didn't like the system.

Although he'd agreed in principle to sign when he was fourteen he wasn't bound, and with what seemed like impeccable timing Coventry City approached him. Jack Nicholls was the local scout who lived in Wallsend and he came with the huge figure of Mr Walton, clocking in at some fifteen stone. It was the size of Mr Walton and the fact that they took him down to Coventry in a blue MK 1 Escort that made the biggest impression on the boy. Once there he'd train with the schoolboys, play in odd practice matches and generally demonstrate his skills.

Sheffield United also showed a determination to sign him on as a schoolboy. They took a different approach and invited him down on the train with his parents. The train was packed and the journey seemed endless. Chris was not impressed. They were met by the assistant manager, a Mr Short, who took them around the ground. The club had just bounced back to the First Division and for a while, impressed with the likes of Tony Currie and Alan Woodward (grey before his time), they were the League's pacemakers. Chris was more impressed by the set-up than the method of transportation and stayed three or four days on his own, the first time he had really been away from home.

Although the digs were nice and the people friendly it was a painful time. Chris was still extremely shy, and could only feel comfortable with people once he got to know them. He had little or no confidence in himself and was not prepared to hold out for a really major club to come to him. He felt hurt and disappointed that his beloved Sunderland had shown no interest and at fourteen almost felt he was on the scrap heap. It was therefore a straight choice between Coventry and Sheffield United and he and his parents sat down for a long talk that they all thought was going to decide his long term future.

Elizabeth and Joseph favoured the Sheffield Club. They liked the fact they'd taken them down and given them all the time they'd wanted to look around and ask questions. Chris, however, leant towards Coventry. There the digs were on top of the ground, the town centre was nearby, the food was good, and all the schoolboys were housed together with the apprentices' digs just across the road. It felt more like the close-knit community he was used to.

Wedding to Lorna Bruce          *Photo: Newcastle Chronicle and Journal Ltd*

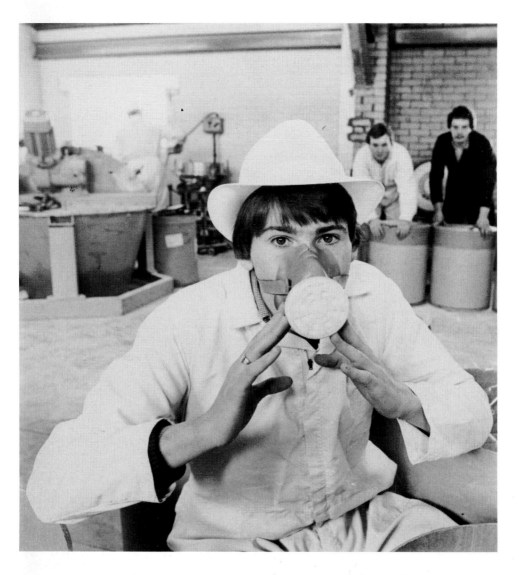

Prepared . . .for a job making seasoning for sausages     *Photo: Rex Features Ltd*

Aged 14 and having signed schoolboy papers with Coventry City
*Photo: Newcastle Chronicle and Journal Ltd*

Midfield trio? The Waddle brothers (Chris far left)

Early footballing days

In action for Newcastle United, 1981

Photo: *Newcastle Chronicle and Journal Ltd*

Chris Waddle, Simon Stainrod (QPR), August 1982          *Photo: Steve Hale*

Gary Williams (Aston Villa), Chris Waddle, September 1984    *Photo: Steve Hale*

Waddle, Megson, Brown, March 1985                    *Photo: Steve Hale*

Chris prevailed and schoolboy terms were signed at the Waddle house in 1974, with Joe proudly filming it.

The *Gateshead Post* featured a photograph of him kicking a ball in the garden and the Waddle Scrapbook had begun. As far as Chris was concerned his formal education was at an end. He regrets it now and urges youngsters to ensure that they don't give up everything for football. His first year report had shown promise; 'Can do better, but the skill is there if he wants to work at it.' He didn't and by the second year there was little encouragement with the third year being terrible. When he speaks to schoolboys nowadays he says, 'just because you've signed, don't give up your education,' but in their response of a disinterested 'yeah' he hears the echo of his own life, a life he thought was his own, but which really has to be shared far beyond that belief.

He certainly is convinced now that he should have waited to sign and commit himself until he was fifteen. If the skill is there then there's really no need to sign schoolboy terms – that merely gives security to the club for very little expense. If a boy waits till he is fifteen he can often have the pick of the top clubs if he's good enough.

The young footballer noticed no immediate change in his lifestyle. There was the odd bit of jealousy amongst his friends, but certainly not in the case of Gary Durham, whose footballing ability was to say the least limited. At about this time Gary met Chris' dad for the first time and without being introduced went up to him at a school match and said, 'I'd be playing, but I can't get into the team at the moment. I'm an Asa Hartford type – a midfield general. Gordon Jago's been up and met my parents.' Joe expressed an interest in this child prodigy and was totally convinced by him. Gary simply smiled, said he was only kidding and moved away. Chris sometimes felt that the only similarity between Gary and Asa Hartford was that one had a hole in his heart, the other a hole in his head.

Not only was his school life coming to a disappointing end but in the last year school football was also disappointing. Before that everything had gone well. The school had always won the League and for the first three years had added the Durham County Cup and the League Cup to their trophy cabinet by way of a clean sweep; but Chris' elevation to League status caused a gap – not a rift, nothing as dramatic as that, but a definite gap. Peter Allen felt it more than most, particularly after Newcastle lost interest in him. He was never nasty about it and indeed was always enthusiastic about

Chris's career, but clearly deep inside he was hurt. Everybody would ask about training and the like, but Peter had nothing to ask. He had been there, he knew.

Chris' brothers were inordinately proud. Joe was into bikes when his kid brother signed up and would bring his wild bike friends down to watch Chris in the street, offering him twenty pence to keep the ball up twenty times. Chris would do it, but rarely got paid although he's sure Joe collected a fortune in bets from his friends. Joseph Senior was over the moon. He'd had high hopes of Ray, but Chris was something else, from the first time he'd really seen him kicking that ball at Newcastle Races at the age of three he'd been a natural with that left foot. For the Waddle hopes of a football dynasty it had been third time lucky and any residuary disappointment that 'Gail' had not appeared finally vanished forever.

Every school holiday found Chris going up to Coventry to train, although they had so many schoolboys on their books that they could only take Chris on alternate weeks. For him that was more than enough for after a couple of days he'd be desperately homesick, tearing his hair out to get back to the North-East.

Mr Walton would arrange his transport, pick him up from his home, then pick up another lad in Durham. From there it was on to collect Ray Godden, who appeared a few times for Coventry first team before going on to Hartlepool after injury and then Worksop. Their final passenger was Danny Thomas. Danny was a delight even then and Chris felt it more than most when his career was brutally brought to an end against QPR. Danny's was the first black face Chris had seen outside of the pits where eventually it always washed off. He was a bubbly personality and even when Chris played for Newcastle Reserves later in his career against Coventry Danny made a point of coming into the dressing room after the match and asking how Chris was getting on, that some four years after a passing acquaintance between a couple of schoolboys.

Chris found the Coventry experience hard going. It was in a way like moving up to University from school. At school you may have been one of the brightest in the class but at University everybody was one of the brightest. During the week they'd train and play practice games, often against the apprentices who included Gary Thompson and Paul Dyson both destined to break through into the first team. Chris played on the left wing even then but coming up against skilful right-backs he was given no opportunity to shine. The homesickness didn't help. He didn't really want to live away from home and in a house of ten or twelve schoolboys, his shyness was only accentuated when he found very little to do. It was then he began to develop his real talent of watching television. The days settled into their own routine; training, television, bed. There was no real thought of girls and an exciting night out was to go into town to the cinema which Chris did only once in his entire time in Coventry.

Chris stuck it out until he was fifteen but then realised it wasn't for him and it seemed for a while that the Chris Waddle career was over before it ever really started.

# Chapter 8

In Chris' final year at school he was offered the opportunity of work experience. He quite quietly told them that the only work he knew or wanted was football and he was quite happy to gain any more experience in that field the school thought appropriate. The school was not impressed and after a lengthy cross examination of the boy discovered he liked cars and, with that unvarying logic that belongs to teachers, Chris was designated to gain work experience as a motor mechanic on the electrical side. It was a dubious decision and one that does not lend itself kindly to an action replay.

From eight in the morning till four-thirty in the afternoon Chris worked with a very grumpy electrician and his eccentric apprentice who owned sixty TV sets and was obsessed by technology. The electrician had the same attitude as the elderly Chris should have visited on his community service – namely that Chris was unasked for and unnecessary. Consequently his main function became passing the tools to the apprentice until he was entrusted with fitting a bulb into a rear light of a vehicle. What he remembers most about the job was how cold it was in the garage, a huge barn of a place filled with lorries. The two other boys who accompanied Chris were very keen but to the aspiring footballer it seemed like a lifetime prison sentence. Even though he had done very little he felt absolutely shattered at the end of a day, physically and mentally drained by the boredom and the hopelessness of it all. At the end of his period, Chris got a £2 tip, one lad nothing and the third £10. That third boy Keith Burdis, an old friend of Chris' was a useful centre-half who lived in Pelaw. He was offered a job at the garage when he left school and is still there to this day.

The fate, or future, of Keith Burdis highlighted the difference between Chris and other boys of his age. Keith was doing what he wanted to do within the framework of what he felt to be a proper and secure job in the North-East. Without conceit, without any snobishness Chris just felt he was different, that he could do better, that whatever else there was that sort of job and security simply was not for him.

At that time he still had his links with Coventry. It is worth looking a little more closely at how that relationship came to an end as it illustrates so very clearly the vagaries, the selfishness, the mental brutality of professional football. Chris was only 5' 4', under nine stone and seemingly going nowhere. The lads he was playing with were like men and he was intimidated by them. Coventry had said in April 1975 'come down for a month and we'll have a good look at you'. They'd written to the school and asked for permission and the school had responded with alacrity. Their pupil was not taking any exams and they were in favour of anything that might find him a job and improve their school leaving employment statistics.

Chris went on a Saturday with a slight thigh strain. Bob Dennison was in charge and told the boy there was a match on Sunday. Chris told him about his injury and that he didn't think he should play. Dennison was less than happy and instead of suggesting some treatment at the club Chris found himself home by tea-time on Sunday. His parents were even less happy at the club's attitude. Months drifted on and it was not until Chris had left school in fact that he even heard from Coventry. Mr Walton, at least, had the courtesy to 'phone personally. He told Chris that there were no apprenticeships left but if he wanted to come up at Christmas and try again he'd be welcome – or else the club would release him. As soon as he said that Chris decided that they couldn't be that interested and so he asked for his release which was duly given. Nobody filmed the release and there was no article in the *Gateshead Post*.

Obviously professional football clubs have to be selective and cannot sign on as full-time players every schoolboy or apprentice who passes through their ranks. Yet there must be a kinder way of dealing with this issue than that adopted by many clubs. They should realise the psychological scars they are inflicting on a young man, with limited education whose dreams are shattered and who enters the nightmare of the unemployment queue. It is to be hoped that clubs will employ a properly trained individual who can deal with these boys and young men, not only in explaining to them why their futures do not lie with the particular club, but also in assisting and encouraging them either to find a position elsewhere in football or else guiding them into another career. It is a debt football owes to those who support the game and one it almost totally ignores.

Chris wasn't dead yet, though, not by a long shot. There is a resilient streak in him, almost a stubborn streak which is only apparent when you really get to know him. A friend in the street knew Charlie Ferguson, a well respected scout whose main claim to fame was that he'd discovered Bobby Kerr who'd led Sunderland to that famous 1973 Cup Final victory. Now that same Charlie Ferguson asked Chris to come to train on Tuesdays and Thursdays. Hope rose anew. Perhaps the Newcastle, Sheffield United and Coventry fiascos had merely been stepping stones, tests sent by some greater power, on the way to his grand ambition to play for the team he'd always wanted. It was not to be. There was little difference at Sunderland from the training he'd found at Newcastle and after attending four times up to the end of the season he was not asked back and he heard nothing more.

Not that there was any great shortage of football in his life. On Saturday afternoons he was playing for Pelaw Juniors and on Sunday he was appearing for Whitehouse Social Club in Washington a team for which his brother Ray also played. Eventually he decided that was too far to travel and Peter Allen's father, who worked for HMH Printing Company, invited Chris via Peter to join the work team and once more he took the field alongside his old friend. The manager of that side claimed to have some involvement with Charlton Athletic although neither Chris nor anybody else ever found out precisely what that involvement was. The most outstanding thing about the side was the goalkeeper, a real extrovert called Alfie who Chris recalls as being totally mad. It's also of passing interest to note that his daughter has been out with Tottenham's newly signed star Paul Gascoigne.

That team folded when Chris was asked to join Mount Pleasant Social Club by Alfie McKay who ran the junior team on Saturdays. It was a pub team of which the teenage Chris was by far its youngest member. Alfie McKay was another interesting character, and the team's results reflected that. They'd win 5-4, lose 7-5, whilst the small rotund figure of Alfie McKay always wearing his little woollen hat, yelled and screamed a mixture of encouragement and abuse on the touch line. Alfie who would bring young lads down from the junior team and gradually integrate them into the Sunday side, was probably the first real manager under whom Chris played. Alfie was unmarried, lived with his mother and was simply football crazy. For him it was a total and fulfilling passion. At this time Peter Allen seemed to be overtaking Chris in terms of their footballing careers, and he was asked to play for the local champions Clarke Chapman.

Results for both of Chris' teams continued to be erratic. Pelaw juniors once lost 17-1 with Chris getting their goal. That same season they were drawn against Eppleton in the Cup. A suitable simile for the fixture might be Grange Hill versus Eton. Eppleton had a lot of tradition and a fine ground. Pelaw were the 'dead end kids' who even hired a battered mini bus to take the team and some fifteen supporters to the match. The supporters wasted no time in telling everybody within earshot how good a team they were.

The Eppleton stadium was so sophisticated that it even had a fence around it – something unheard of in a league where if goal posts were left up overnight, they were likely to be stolen. One of the Pelaw supporters, togged out in his best Doc Martens, climbed the fence, ran across the pitch unfurling a Newcastle flag and with a bloodcurdling yell of 'Geordies' began digging up the wet grass. The snooty Eppleton crowd took a deep breath and stood back in amazement and horror. As it was, that was the only mark Pelaw made in the afternoon as, apart from changing ends, they failed to get out of their own half. They were forced into the unusual formation of two left-backs, two right-backs and everybody else in central defence. They finally lost 9-0 without so much as forcing a corner, and felt themselves lucky that they were let off so lightly. At the end the Pelaw team just looked at each other, laughed and gave three cheers for Eppleton, with their supporters singing, 'We'll support you evermore'.

Those were the weekends. During the week Chris' school career was grinding to a close. On the Friday before Easter 1977, when he was sixteen-and-a-half, he, like a dozen or so others, was taking no exams. There was nothing to keep him there any longer, indeed there had never really been anything to keep him there. With the other academic no-hopers a race was organised to see who could get out of school first. Chris won and headed straight off to Holly Hill, the site of the local unemployment office. He told them he'd just left school and the following Thursday morning Chris Waddle, England-International-to-be, signed on the dole.

# CHAPTER 9

His first pay cheque by way of unemployment benefit was £10.30. At first he'd sign on on Thursday mornings, get his cheques on Saturdays, and then it was down to the Post Office to cash it. As time went by, however, he found it more and more difficult even to get up to collect his money. His friend Alan Burdis was in an even worse position. He was three years older than Chris and had been out of work for years. The two lads would tramp disconsolately around all the factories in the area asking if there was any work available but the answer always came back 'no'. Although Chris has never been a political animal, the seeming insensitivity of the system made him begin to understand his father's point of view even though his father had never experienced the frustration that was now facing the son.

There were only a few weeks left to the end of the season and no offers were raining in from the likes of Liverpool, Manchester United or Everton, nor indeed from Hartlepool or Darlington. Looking back it is quite amazing how a talent such as Chris' could have escaped the net, and one is left wondering how many other young Chris Waddles are queuing up with their UB 40s.

The weeks took on a dull routine. Monday there was nothing, then on Tuesday there was Hewarth Youth Club which cost all of 10p admission. There Chris, and dozens in the same position as him would play snooker, darts and table-tennis or simply listen to the music. Gary Durham also attended the club. He had been more fortunate than Chris and had an apprenticeship with Dewhurst, although had his reputation preceeded him it is hardly likely they would have entrusted him with anything sharper than a blunt razor blade, let alone a butcher's knife! The youth club itself had half a dozen more genteel and intellectual members who were into pottery. Chris and Gary were particularly incensed by this because they arranged for everybody to watch little films about pottery. Eventually, in a truly democratic manner the boys imported enough of their friends into the club to outvote the pottery freaks and from then on it was either real films or discos. Once a month the club would be bursting at the seams for a special evening with two hundred or more people there. One of them was a fourteen year old called Lorna Bruce.

Chris at sixteen was beginning to develop his own style. He'd wear a green and white Celtic shirt (having overcome his schoolboy aversion to the colours) with a Rangers badge to avoid any accusation of religious bias. These were topped off by a cut-off wrangler jacket with Sunderland patches, together with a pair of jeans or pleated trousers showing the regulatory gap to his Doc Martens. Elizabeth Waddle would take the trousers up for him without enthusiasm, but fortunately for parental calm at home he never sported a skinhead haircut. One night Chris was feeling particularly smart in a new Crombie overcoat with a red handkerchief. A *Montrose* album was playing when a girl appeared at Chris' side. 'Are you seeing anybody?' she asked above the din with Northern directness. Chris shook his head. 'My friend Lorna Bruce would like to see you.' Chris shook his head again. 'No. I don't want to see anybody.' Chris didn't even bother to find out which one Lorna was. He simply didn't feel sufficiently independent to get involved with any girl. Independence is a word that is written large in Chris' dictionary. Not to be beholden, to support himself without charity, simply by using his natural skills and talents. So many other professionals simply grasp what's on offer from potential hangers-on. Chris is not like that. He chooses to spend his time with people he likes and respects, not those who only want to know him and give to him because of what he does.

Despite the despair humour kept on peeking through. Chris and his friends were accustomed to hanging around the streets on non-club evenings. They still played the same games they'd played as children, knocking on people's doors and running away, sometimes being chased by the householders for as long as an hour. Then on Guy Fawkes night, Gary Durham had an idea. That in itself should have been warning enough. One of them would be dressed up as a guy with a Parka and be used to collect money. Inevitably Chris was selected and duly dumped outside somebody's house. All that happened was that he got kicked to pieces, generally beaten up whilst no money at all was received and Gary, hiding in the shadows, was doubled up with laughter.

For the most part, however, there was real boredom, alleviated only when he either played or went to see football. He'd had a brief flirtation with Newcastle before he was fourteen when he got free tickets, but after he'd left the club he felt disinclined to pay to watch them play and would generally go to Sunderland with Keith Mullen.

The first away game he ever saw was at Hull in October 1974 when Sunderland lost 3-1 and Chris stood on the terraces taunting the Hull supporters whose team were nicknamed the 'Tigers' with cries of 'Pussycats.' Later that same season Chris was doing a paper round and listening to a thriller between Manchester United who topped the League and Sunderland in second place. A crowd of 66,000 were there that day to see United win 3-2. Chris was extremely upset whenever Sunderland lost and that day more so than usual. He was not then, and is not now, one to take defeat gracefully. After Arsenal knocked Spurs out of the Littlewoods Cup Semi-Final in 1987, he simply would not talk to anybody, Lorna included for 48 hours.

As a consolation for Sunderland's defeat he offered Keith Mullen, who'd come to his house, an Oxo. Keith thought he was going to get a hot drink but instead all he got was a raw Oxo cube which Chris would eat by the dozen, picking at them bit by bit, making a whole meal out of the one little square. He had another friend, Barry Charlton, with similar tastes and would buy them 120 at a time. Keith Mullen thought the Waddle household was mad.

The trouble about travelling to see Sunderland was that everywhere (except Newcastle) was a long journey. However, with two or three pounds given to him by his mother Chris would often make the journey even when still at school. Vic Halom was his hero although most of the boys also liked Billy Hughes. When Billy was rumoured to be about to leave Roker Park Keith and Chris waited for him after the match to get the news straight from the horse's mouth.

'Hello, Bill, you all right?' the boys asked. He grunted a monosyllabic reply in a broad Scottish accent.

'You don't really want to leave do you Billy?'

'I want to get as far away from here as possible,' he replied. End of conversation.

In the 1975/76 season Chris and Keith attended all the home games. When Sunderland beat York 4-1 Chris pinched a Union Jack that was going spare at the end given to the Sunderland fans. Somebody simply abandoned it and Chris wondered why. However, when he opened it up and looked at it in the coach he realised it was the biggest flag he'd ever seen. He tried to wrap it around himself but it would just trail on the floor. Eventually he in turn abandoned it to somebody else. He did not go to many away games. At Blackburn there were about two thousand North-Easterners and a few numbers of them pursued three Blackburn supporters, two of whom were badly beaten up with the other leaping over a small wall and swimming across the river for his safety. It was Chris' first real view of soccer violence. He took note and was sickened by it, yet it in no way affected his fanaticism for Sunderland, who eventually went to the top of the League after a 4-0 win over Notts County.

It was nothing in those days for Sunderland to take eight or ten thousand supporters away. On the 1st February 1975 Chris went on a school trip to Blackpool. Billy Hughes missed a penalty and Micky Walsh scored a memorable goal on *Match of the Day* which became Goal of the Season. Blackpool's usual home gate was eight and a half thousand but that day it topped sixteen and a half.

The following season, too, he religiously followed Sunderland. He went all the way to Norwich and saw them fall two behind until Rowell pulled one back, and then Bobby Kerr coming on as a substitute got an equaliser. That match was particularly memorable because he'd especially bought a big bicycle hooter for the game which was promptly taken off him at the entrance gate by the officials. He was told to collect it after the match but as that meant wading through the entire Norwich crowd he decided discretion was the better part of valour and that his health was more important than an unused £2 hooter. Despite a six hour trip to Norfolk, Sunderland took ten thousand supporters with them.

The match against Arsenal was an eye opener. Many Newcastle supporters had joined the crowd taunting their former hero Malcolm MacDonald. The unmerciful gibes at Supermac continued for the whole ninety minutes and it was Chris' first experience of the way Newcastle treated their expatriot heroes, a treatment which he was to receive himself many years later. Curiously Chris did not attend the local derby against Newcastle that season which Newcastle won 2-0, he was simply too frightened. After that match Sunderland slumped to the bottom of the League playing ten games without a goal and the manager put in the kids such as Kevin Arnott, Ashurst, Gary Rowell, Alan Brown, and Shaun Elliott. The team began to win and although there were four consecutive successes against Bristol City, Middlesborough, West Bromwich and West Ham, it was really too late. For the final match of the season there were 36,000 at

Everton compared to the 20,000 who had seen Everton play West Bromwich the week before and 25,000 who saw them play Newcastle the week after. Sunderland lost 2-0 and Coventry drew with Bristol City, they both stayed up but Sunderland were relegated.

Sunderland's fortunes were on a downward spiral and Chris himself was doing no better. He'd left school in the Easter of 1977 and by the start of the 1977/78 season there had still been no enquiries for him. Then in August 1977 with Sunderland about to embark on a season of Second Division football Chris was actually offered a job interview. It was a fact incidental to his life at the time that one of the teams to be relegated with Sunderland was Tottenham Hotspur.

# CHAPTER 10

The job opportunity was with Cheviot Seasoning Ltd who are not, as has been inaccurately reported in almost every newspaper, sausage makers. In fact the company made seasoning to flavour sausages and pies. The position for which Chris went for his interview was a labouring job, not a trade, but after all those months on the dole anything was better than nothing.

In fact, Chris had seen the Cheviot factory every week from the dole office, but never in his bleakest despair did he think he would end up there. Chris is not familar with the world of Charles Dickens but there is little doubt that the position in which he found himself would have been immediately recognisable to any Dickens hero.

His brother Joe took him to the interview on his Suzuki bike. The Cheviot factory was on an industrial estate. There was JR Dalziel, the meat importers with their huge freezers filled with carcasses, then a unit selling butcher's utensils and right at the end the seasoning plant. The first thing that hit him was the smell. 'What is this place?' was all that Chris could say. It was indeed like another world. Jenny George the secretary there showed him in to see Dick Swailes. Dick sat there and explained the job while Chris struggled unsuccessfully to remove his crash helmet, finally giving up and sitting throughout the interview like a spaceman. He thought he had no chance of getting the job but two days later he received a 'phone call, was offered the position and dubiously accepted. Later he and Dick had a good laugh about the boy who sat through the entire interview wearing a crash helmet.

His starting salary was £20, which netted down to £13.80 after tax, insurance etc. This meant that he was getting for a full week's work £3.50 more than he had been receiving on the dole. A few of his more fortunate friends had obtained apprenticeships, and they were getting the same money. Chris teased them gently but by the time he left Cheviot, two-and-a-half years later, his pay packet had gone up to a meagre £40, whilst those who had seen their time out were receiving a real living wage. It took a while until they looked at Chris' Superstar salary with real envy. Perhaps Chris' apprenticeship was just a little bit longer than anybody else's.

When the disillusioned young footballer started at Cheviot they employed only Dick Swailes, Jenny George and David Rocks. What the company really did was to make flavouring in 300 lb batches of salt, cayenne, coriander and basil mixed with the dye and used for seasoning. The ingredients may have had romantic names but the result was anything but that.

The job itself was hardly challenging, consisting of bibs and bobs. David Rocks would drive the forklift and Chris would regard it as the high point of his day when he was allowed to do so. For the most part however, he would stand at the foot of the blender, judging when enough of the mixture had shot down to fill a 56 lb box. In between that he'd sweep up or glue the boxes together. Although he was grateful for the job he could not help but think it was the end of the world.

The smell of the dust began to get down his throat and he'd come home spitting red phlegm. If he'd spent his whole life in the job he had little doubt that it would have destroyed his lungs and killed him as surely as a life down the mines. Eventually they gave him a mask to prevent the dust getting to him but all it really did was make him look like 'Miss Piggy' and leave marks on his head at the end of the day which made it impossible for him to go out socially straight from work without feeling selfconscious. The nickname they gave to the skinny kid who was still not more than 5' 4' tall did nothing to lift his confidence – 'Grasshopper', they called him. One day they asked him to fetch a bag of salt. So bored was he from gluing boxes and sweeping the floor that he ran keenly to pick up the bag. It was only then he realised it weighed 50 lbs and as he put it on his shoulders he simply collapsed. There were eight or nine steps to negotiate but he couldn't move and eventually David Rocks had to assist and he finished up doubling up with laughter.

After a while Chris' honesty and perseverance won through in a minor victory and he was allowed to do the same tasks as David. Rocks was a Newcastle fanatic who played for the Dalziel teams and they had many a football argument which helped to pass the day. Just as when he had been unemployed, his life slipped into a drab routine – work throughout the week, then out with the same group of friends on Friday night, Saturday night to Pelaw social club and Sunday mornings when he didn't play football he'd play Bingo hoping to win that last house of £50.

Before he went to work Chris had rarely drunk. In fact he prided himself on 'never being seen with a drink.' Then he had something not to drink for, because drink affected his fitness to play football, and might affect his chance of the major break through. Now he was not averse to the lunchtime drink with David. However, he rarely got drunk – that is until Pelaw Juniors hired a hall and booked a band called 'Goldie'. The group had been booked well in advance and by the time of the dance in May 1978 they were at No 7 in the charts, their one and only success. The club was absolutely packed and Chris and his friend David Cox got really stuck into Special Federation Brew, so stuck in that he has no recollection of how he got home. Elizabeth couldn't wake him up the next morning and told a 'white lie' to Cheviot by claiming he had 'flu'; but as David Rocks drank in the club all the time Chris thinks it fooled nobody. Eventually when he could get off the bed without falling over he went to see Gary Durham. 'Never again' he swore.

Later that week he and David Cox tried to catch Joseph Waddle's attention at the Station (now the Pelaw Inn) – his Dad's regular watering hole. Chris was only 17 and tapped on the window of the snug where his dad sat. His father beckoned him in and the barman turned a blind eye and served them with two lagers. Unfortunately there was no escaping the all seeing eye of Gary Durham. 'This is the lad who'd never be seen with a drink in his hand – what happened to never again?' he taunted. As it happens Chris was as good as his word and never allowed himself to get into that condition again.

Gradually be became more confident. Instead of crawling home exhausted each night he'd have enough energy to go out with the lads, to play pool to listen to music or best of all on Wednesday nights to train with Pelaw Juniors. Although he did not realise it at the time his work was a far more rigorous training programme than any he was likely to meet at a professional club. He was also still playing Saturday afternoons and Sunday mornings. When the time came for Chris to play football for a living he would be more than ready. For the moment though nobody was inviting him to join the party.

The only party he attended was with 'The Gang' – there was Keith Smith, nicknamed 'Hendo' – a diabetic who lived only for weekends, the infamous Gary Durham, Aiden Burrel – 'Bub', the butt of everybody's teasing, Keith Mullen and Peter Allen. Together the boys would go into the City Centre on a Friday night and queue to get into a bar, then Sundays would mean a visit to the Northern Soul Night at the Mayfair – the Mecca club in Newcastle. At 6.30 pm they'd catch the bus from Pelaw, nervous on the first occasion that they wouldn't be admitted. As it was their money was as good as anybody else's and they were nodded in without the bouncers on the door giving them more than a cursory glance.

The second time it was different, 'how old are you?' they asked Chris. He'd been rehearsing his date of birth all the way there and told them with confidence. 'Away and get your birth certificate,' was the reply. It was the only time he was not admitted as thereafter every Sunday he'd don his Fred Perry shirt and trousers and stand swaying to the recorded wall of sound that featured the same records over and over again – Jimmy James and the Bandits' *Breaking Down the Walls of Heartache* being one of the favourites. The boys would always be there before nine to get cheaper admission and as the drink flowed and the music pounded out would dance on their own. It must have been a terrifying sight to behold over 200 young Geordies dressed in their 40'' bottomed, pleated baggy trousers leaping up and down oblivious even of each other.

The gang, Chris included, were becoming more and more clothes conscious, but clothes required money. Keith Smith – Hendo – was getting a relatively decent wage and discovered that was the key to opening a credit account at Top Shop. When they saw Hendo in his new clothes every Sunday they all decided to follow his lead. Economics was none of their strong points and the interest they were paying meant that their accounts were never getting any less. Eventually faced with a bill of £100 or more, Chris in desperation borrowed money from his mother to pay it off. It was a hard harsh world outside of Pelaw and one for which Chris was as yet, totally unprepared.

# CHAPTER 11

On Sunday mornings Chris was now playing for Pelaw Social Club. At the time of his selection for his first game Pelaw were unbeaten. Chris' entry into the side was heralded with a 5-1 thrashing by the team at the top of the league and as Chris sat head in hands in the dressing room, he heard more than one senior player mutter 'good decision' in respect of his selection. There were twelve more games in the season and Chris got the man of the match award in eight of them and then shared the player of the year trophy. Not for the last time in his career he'd silenced his critics in the best possible way – on the field.

Pelaw Social Club also made the cup final. With the score at 2-2 Chris saw the opposing goalie miskick. The ball ran out to the young Waddle who chipped the 'keeper perfectly, the ball landed dead on the goal line and the wind promptly blew it back on to the field. Into extra time and Pelaw were awarded a corner. Chris dragged his tired limbs over to take it, hit it into the box and even today can remember praying, 'please let it go in.' The Pelaw centre-half ran in, met the ball perfectly, and Pelaw had won. It was a night of celebration and several rounds of Carlsberg Special Brew almost made Chris forget his promise never again to become legless.

Chris' performances were attracting a lot of local interest and half way through the season Clarke Chapman, the most prestigious amateur team in the area, invited Chris to join them. They were a Saturday team who already had Peter Allen playing for them in goal and so once again the two friends took the field together. When Chris joined them the left and right wing berths were already adequately filled and Chris was slotted into the side in the left midfield. The team rarely lost. The striker was Keith McNall who moved onto Gateshead, and Graham Hood played alongside him. Graham's dad was a Bolton scout whose professional opinion was that Chris would never make it. Every so often he'd take some of the Clarke Chapman boys to Bolton for a trial, but Chris was never selected. His son, Graham, however, went down every time for yet another trial but finally ended up at Crook Town. Mickey Wilden had been on Bolton's books, had been offered an apprenticeship and declined. Chris recalls him as being able to hit the ball harder than anyone else he ever knew. Mickey could have gone all the way in the game but he was ever ready for a fight and was unreliable, turning up for a game or for training when he chose. Success in football is not just a matter of skill – it's temperament and discipline as well. Mark McGurkin who had been in Chris' class at school for six years was the centre-half. All in all it was as near to a professional set-up as could be found outside the professional game.

Chris thrived on the challenge. He started growing and sprang up to nearly six foot although he was still very thin. Played in a variety of positions from sweeper, through the midfield and sometimes on the right wing his game also began to grow in its technique and experience. At the end of the 1977/78 season he was confident enough to think he was ready to get back into the professional game. Not yet eighteen, but already thinking of a come back!

Clarke Chapman always held an end of season party and there Chris was formally asked if he'd like to sign up with the senior side. He replied by saying he was looking for a team who would pay him some money to top up his wages. Jim Callagham, the team physiotherapist who had first invited him for a trial overheard the conversation. Obviously he'd seen something in the boy that others had overlooked because he realised that Chris could go further than Clarke Chapman although perhaps he did not then realise quite how much further. Jim told Chris to leave it to him but by the time Chris was due to go on holiday he'd still not heard anything.

He and David Cox went off to Benidorm. It was Chris' first trip abroad and he hated every minute of it. Even today he has no patience for sitting out in the sun as he tends to go red rather than brown. All he remembers of that holiday was that it was just too hot to play football on the beach. He couldn't wait to get back to see if there was any news for him from Jim Callagham's contacts. There was. Billy Bell had taken over at Tow Law who played in the Drysborough Northern League and on Callagham's recommendation Chris was invited to train with them at the end of the summer of 1978.

He had attended only one or two training sessions on Tuesdays when he was told there was a friendly away to Frickley on a Thursday. The manager told him to come along, 'oh, and bring your boots, in case we're short.' Chris didn't need to be told twice. They picked him up in a minibus in Gateshead and sure enough there were only eleven and Chris was playing. Once he saw the ground his enthusiasm waned a little for overlooking the pitch was the most enormous slag heap he had ever seen which looked as if it might slip at any moment. In fact it held fast, Tow Law drew 2-2 and Chris marked his debut by scoring one and making one. One of his team mates that day was Ray Ellison, who had played for Newcastle and Sunderland, and was possibly the last captain of Workington Town before they left the League. His incessant running and enthusiasm for the game made the other players ask just one question, 'where did he come from?'

By the start of the season he was in the first team and earning the princely sum of £5 a match. Meanwhile he was also still playing for Pelaw Social Club. Ray Waddle, his brother was turning out for Leam Lane Social Club whose record was played eight and lost eight, as opposed to Pelaw's record of one loss in eight matches. Ray exerted some fraternal pressure and asked Chris to transfer across. Chris, not for the first or last time in his life could not let somebody close to him down and agreed with the result that nobody at Pelaw ever spoke to Ray again.

Chris, however, was under contract to Tow Law even if he was only being paid a pittance and should not have played Sunday football at all. He hurt his ankle and scared to tell the club strapped it up and turned out for Leam Lane in a 5-0 victory where he scored three and made two; but his transfer was too late to stop Leam Lane's relegation. Despite crowds of 200, they still went down.

The summer of 1978 was memorable in another respect; Chris really met Lorna Bruce for the first time. The Sunday night discos would finish at midnight, whilst the last train would leave at 11.40 pm. Every Sunday therefore meant a mad dash to the station until one night they arrived just in time to wave goodbye to the train pulling away. There was an all-night bus but it took one and a half hours going round the whole of the North-East dropping off the late night revellers. Lorna and a friend also arrived late and met Chris and his friends as they came up from the platform to tell them the bad news. Chris watched with some envy as Lorna confidently hailed a taxi, not realising she was the same girl who had sent him a message. Now interested he actually asked Keith Mullen her name. 'Do you fancy her?' Keith asked. 'Nah,' Chris replied, then to emphasise the point, 'nah, definitely not.'

Of the gang, Dill had bought a car – a Ford Escort Mark 1, a real banger without even the luxury of floor boards, a model straight out of 'The Flintstones' as Chris himself recalls. Chris was driving with Dill when they saw Lorna at Hewarth and offered her a lift home. Chris plucked up courage to ask if she would see him but it was her turn to play it cool and she said she didn't know. On the following Sunday they both went to the Mayfair and Chris asked Peter Allen to ask her again if she'd see him. To Chris' disbelief the reply was yes and he sat with her the whole evening, neither of them saying very much. Lorna now claims she was forced into seeing Chris because so many people were asking her about it, but there is little doubt that they were always meant for each other. Chris still had so little confidence in the relationship that he took Gary Durham with him on their first date in case she didn't turn up!

At that time Lorna was just starting work at De La Rue's. She would see him some nights but at other times would put him off, claiming she did not want to get too serious. Chris felt she was generally playing with his affections. She would pack him in on a Sunday and then be back with him a week later. Chris bought her little presents, in particular one terrible pair of earrings from Spain which she said she'd never wear – but did. Romance was a dubious word to use up in the North-East. You were 'seeing' somebody or 'going' with them, but you were never in love, or if you were you didn't make a public statement on the issue.

# CHAPTER 12

Billy Bell took the management of Tow Law Football Club very seriously. There were two training sessions a week for the first team, Monday and Wednesday. Monday was hard running and Wednesday was coaching. Bell had started at Evenwood where he was totally unknown and had inspired them to win a cup in the league. Wherever he went he had a set pattern of play. The goalkeeper would throw it to the full-back, he'd play it to the left midfield man who'd gone wide, Chris would go short and if he was marked the ball would be hit up to the centre-forward; if Chris was unmarked he got the ball. It was all very tactical for that level of play and not many teams were able to close it down completely. Bell got Tow Law on a cup run and eventually they went out to Brandon 4-0 in the second qualifying round of the 79/80 season while Brandon themselves went on to the third round proper only to lose 3-0 to Bradford City.

Blyth Spartan were the real high flyers of North-Eastern Non-League football and they always represented Tow Law's biggest game of the season. Although Tow Law lost 2-0 to them Joe Harvey, Newcastle's ex-manager and scout had been there to watch Chris and was sufficiently impressed to come back with Basil Hayward and watch him again. Barnsley and Rotherham had also been eyeing him, as had Sunderland who indeed asked Tow Law if they could have him on a week's trial to play against a Brazilian team. Tow Law said no, he was under contract to them, and they were suddenly becoming aware they were sitting on a potentially hot property.

After one game in December 1979 when Chris particularly shone Joe Harvey finally approached him after the final whistle and said he wanted to sign him for Newcastle. Chris was too polite to point out they'd already signed him once. He was invited to St James' Park on New Year's Day 1980 when Newcastle had a local derby against Sunderland. He was told to see Billy McGarry but it was Geoff Allen, the youth team manager who came to talk to him. He told the boy that Mr McGarry was very busy and in fact didn't have time to see him and perhaps it would be better if things were left for a bit. For the second time in his short career Newcastle had let Chris down. The cock was to crow a third time. It seemed a long journey back with Billy Bell who'd come to keep him company and even worse he'd seen his beloved Sunderland lose 3-1 on a hard frosty pitch.

As fast as he was being knocked down there seemed to be something to pick him up again before he became a side show coconut once more. This time the pick me up came in the shape of Sunderland when Charlie Ferguson, their Chief Scout, asked him down for a two week trial. In order to get it in Chris had to take his summer holiday in January, but having arranged that with his employer, off he went wearing a purple track suit bottom. It was his bad luck that in the friendly against Gateshead for which he was selected the opposing full-back was Stephen Higgins who'd played with him right through school. He knew Waddle's game inside out and one or two determined tackles destroyed Chris' confidence to dribble. None of the Sunderland players would pass to him and Chris spent a miserable ninety minutes. At the end of the fortnight Frank Clarke told the lad that Ken Knighton and the manager wanted to see him. It was a short, sharp and not very sweet interview. 'You're not really better than what we've got – there's others on the books who look better prospects.'

It was back to Tow Law. On the Tuesday there was a match against the unlikely named Billingham Symphonia. Chris simply couldn't motivate himself to get involved. After ten minutes of despair Billy Bell went mad and took his young player off. On that evening Chris decided to pack it in once and for all. He felt too bruised by the game's injustices to continue. Billy Bell was not the sort of man to stand for that.

'Come on son, prove them wrong. You've got it.'

Motivated again by his manager Chris started playing very well and had a 'phone call from Allan Clarke, then manager of Barnsley inviting Chris to meet him at Scotch Corner. Once more Chris' hopes rose as he thought a contract would be waiting on the cafe table. In fact all he was offered was a two week trial. Chris said no. It took a lot of courage for the shy player to tell the ex-England international but somehow or other he managed it. He couldn't take any more time off work and risk losing his hard sought job. Barnsley would have to take him or leave him. They left him.

He plummeted to the depths again. For the quiet sensitive boy to have had so many rebuffs, so many disappointments must have been earth shattering, yet somehow or other he got to the end of a disappointing season where Tow Law finished twelfth out of twenty and saw their trophy aspirations end with defeat at Stalybridge Celtic. Then with perverse sadism Newcastle 'phoned again. They said they still wanted to sign him but Tow Law wanted £12,000 because they needed floodlights. That was something Chris was to remember some years later when the Tribunal adjudicated his fee on the transfer to Tottenham Hotspur. His contract was up with Tow Law anyway and Blue Star from the same league were interested, offering him £18 per week. Tow Law made him an increased offer of £15 per week but Newcastle topped them with a massive salary of £70 per week!

Chris knew that Joe Harvey and Geoff Allen had been pushing Bill McGarry to sign him but he'd still not met McGarry until the day he signed. He was offered a twelve month contract at that generous £70 per week and without any agents, without any solicitor or accountant present he signed up without even bothering to read what was put before his nose.

The *Evening Chronicle* in Newcastle reported the signing with the headline 'United get teenage striker'. The article went on to say that United had tried to get Waddle the previous season … 'but they were unable to complete the deal'. It was early days yet, of little significance, but already the press were misreporting.

The hardest part was going back to Cheviot to give in his notice. David Rocks had been sacked partially at least because he'd tried to get Chris a rise. When David went Chris said he was going too but the management persuaded him otherwise by bringing in somebody to work under him, a 6' 7'' giant who arrived at work covered in love bites in a Marina in which he claimed he did wheel spins at 70 mph. Dalziels then brought in another man to try and give Dick Swailes a rest and allow him to concentrate on his seasoning. The new arrival lived in a three bedroomed semi and was proud to declare he drove at 50 mph on motorways. He didn't hit it off with anybody and when Dick refused to surrender his recipe book the new man ended up working alongside Chris and the other lads. They would delight in having him at the bottom of the shute, while they opened a full box of dye to topple down, ignoring his cries of 'stop.'

Robert McGee, nicknamed 'Meg', had been in Lorna's year at school and also worked with Chris. He replaced him as the young

# WADDLE

Grasshopper of the company and remained with them for many years. It was that sort of firm.

Chris was always grateful to the Seasoning Company for giving him a job and, as he said to Dick when he told him of Newcastle's offer, he'd always hoped that one day he would leave to play football for a living, but he had never believed it would ever really happen. It was typical of Chris that he asked Bill McGarry if he could miss the first two weeks training of the 1980/81 season so that he could work out his notice. Chris Waddle never forgets to whom he owes a debt, nor does he ever fail to repay it.

# CHAPTER 13

The 1980/81 season hardly heralded Chris Waddle in with a fanfare. Newcastle United had finished ninth in the second division in the season before and with the signing of Kevin Keegan not even a twinkle in a manager's eye they looked set for a lengthy stay in the lower reaches of the League. The fact that Chris joined alongside Alan Shoulder – ex-Blyth Spartans – Peter Cartwright ex-North Shields and Steve Carney also ex-Blyth did not give any great indication of the footballing pedigree or spending ambitions of the club.

In any event it was hard going right from the very start. After the first training session Chris could hardly walk and Alan Oliver a leading North-Eastern Sports Journalist wrote after seeing him play in a friendly against Consett that 'it looks like Newcastle have signed another dud.' Chris then turned out against Blyth, Spennymore and Tow Law all of which were won before the first team came back from its pre-season tour of Sweden.

On August 16th 1980 Chris Waddle made his first appearance for Newcastle in a professional competitive match against Manchester United in the Central League, a Manchester United team containing Andy Ritchie and Ray Wilkins. In the first five minutes Wilkins nutmegged Chris and the learning process was really under way. The reserves lost 2-0, while the first team also lost by the same score at Sheffield Wednesday. The reserves then faced up to Man City (including Polish World Cup Star Kasma Deyna) and lost 2-1 at home whilst the first team scraped a draw at home to Notts County and then were demolished 4-0 by Bolton.

One goal scored in three matches, seven conceded, one point and virtually bottom of the second division. Time had run out for Bill McGarry and the axe was dropped. McGarry simply vanished. There were no goodbyes, just the fact that one morning somebody else was wearing his yellow training kit and the players knew he wasn't coming back. Rumours were rife as they are every time

# WADDLE

Newcastle changes its manager. Everybody was awaiting the big personality appointment, Jack Charlton, maybe Malcolm Mac-Donald recently invalided out of the game, perhaps Bobby Robson. In fact, as he had done so often in the past Joe Harvey filled in and after a 5-2 win by the Reserves against Leeds where Chris scored twice playing alongside Gary Nicholson up front, he immediately promoted Nigel Walker and John Connelly to the first team who promptly beat Luton 2-1.

Chris was not too concerned by McGarry's departure. He'd barely met the man and his influence on his career was virtually nil. He was on a one year contract and just had to make the best of it. He still hardly spoke to anybody and quietly changed in the 'B' dressing room at Benwell alongside the likes of Brian Ferguson (who went to Chester), Gary Nicholson (who went to Blyth), Kevin Pugh (who ended up at Gateshead), Kevin Carr, Chris Withe, Phil Leaver, John Connelly, Ray Montgomery, David Barton (forced out of the game through injury after being tipped as an England possible) and Kenny Wharton who is still playing for Newcastle seven seasons later.

Geoff Allen was in charge of the reserves. They didn't train with the first team and if it was raining the first team squad took over the gym whilst the reserves had to contend with the elements. Chris really enjoyed Allen's training sessions. He'd be encouraged to roam around up front with Gary Nicholson in five-a-side matches, then there was shooting practice and a lot more running to try to get the factory boy matchfit.

The reserve team was a real Geordie affair yet Chris still made no real friends. He'd come in either by bus or with a lift, do his training rigorously and meticulously and then go home. He found it difficult to change his set way of life. There was a slight difference in so far as he didn't have to get up so early – even today he is not the earliest of risers (although breakfast television has made life easier) but then everybody was a lot fitter than him. In some of the matches, by the second-half he could hardly run and he would collapse on to his bed at home often too tired to watch television, a fact that anybody who knows him today would find hard to believe.

The first team were a world apart. Steve Carney, whose brother was at Tow Law would ask him how he was getting on, but the rest of them would just say 'Good morning'. Stuart Boam, Ray Clarke, Ian Davies, Frans Koenen, Billy Rafferty, Bobby Shinton – all names to conjure with in 1988! Gradually though Chris settled in.

He began to mix with Chris Withe (Peter's younger brother) and Ray Montgomery, a Scots boy whose achievements never lived up to his promise, but it was from the experienced men like Colin Suggett and Terry Hibbitt that he learned the most. Suggett with 86 games for Sunderland, 128 for West Bromwich Albion, 203 for Norwich appeared brilliant to Chris, while Hibbitt in his second spell at St James' Park had been the key to the successful MacDonald-Tudor striking partnership of the mid-seventies and was, like Chris at the time, a totally left footed player.

Suddenly the rumours of the managerial appointment were over. Arthur Cox got the job – Arthur who? to many of the players and the newspapers.

Chris, though remembered him as the skinhead who was assistant manager at Sunderland when they won the cup and welcomed him for his Sunderland connection.

Arthur was born in Southam in Warwickshire and still has a booming Midlands accent. He began life as a Coventry player, but then broke his leg so badly that his career was over at the age of nineteen-and-a-half. Coventry kept him on as coach to the juniors whilst he took a full FA coaching course. His career then covered chief coach at Walsall, assistant to Tommy Docherty at Aston Villa (an unlikely double-act), coach at Halifax, assistant at Sunderland, a brief spell in Turkey and then management with Chesterfield. He is now, of course, manager at Derby, whose gain was ultimately Newcastle's loss. He is still totally filled with admiration for Chris and has approached this book with a nervousness that he never brought to the football field and the pertinent question is 'is he going to say anything bad about me'. Arthur can rest easy for Chris is well aware of the debt he owes him even if it was sometimes paid by blood and sweat.

On his first day Arthur got everybody in a circle and shook hands politely with each player. Everybody called him 'boss' until he got to Steve Carney; 'How you doing Arthur?' he asked, and the ice was broken.

Unlike McGarry, Arthur Cox watched every match he could, first team, reserves and juniors alike. Not only Arthur watched Chris, for he was now starting to get write-ups in the papers. On 21st September 1980 the *News of the World* wrote: 'It would seem United have found something special in Chris Waddle ... A tall, shy lad, he has a twinkling left foot.'

In October of the same year the *Evening Chronicle* told of 'nineteen-year-old Chris Waddle bagging goals for the high flying reserves.' Even the Newcastle first team programme was beginning to sing his praises. In the edition for the goalless draw against West Ham, it included the following: 'One young man who has really impressed me has been Chris Waddle, a striker with excellent ball control and skill.' Then Alan Oliver, who had classified Chris as a 'dud', was big enough to eat his own words when reporting on a 2-0 victory for the reserves over Sheffield Wednesday, he wrote: 'Newcastle manager Arthur Cox played six men with first team experience in his reserve side at St James' Park last night. But they were all upstaged by nineteen-year-old Chris Waddle ... The gangling striker has certainly come on in leaps and bounds since I saw him in a pre-season friendly at Consett ... Like most tall strikers Waddle appears slow, but looks are certainly deceptive. His control is excellent and he is really confident on the ball. And he has perfected the art of dropping his shoulder to glide round an opponent.'

Speaking to the press that same night, Arthur Cox said: 'The boy has improved with every game. If he continues to develop at his present rate he will have a good future in the game. He is breathing down the necks of the senior players and that's a good thing. I don't want him to get the wrong ideas. He could read about himself and imagine he is something more than he is.'

That was typical Arthur Cox. Build them up, but not too high. And all the time he was telling Chris, 'work hard and don't get sick of putting the ball into the net,' and always the incessant, almost rhythmic chant, 'it's not enough, I want more, and more, and more ...'

# CHAPTER 14

As the season progressed the results of the reserves contrasted rudely with those of the first team. Although things had improved under Cox, between September 20th and December 13th Newcastle played 15 matches and won only four of them scoring just ten goals. Meanwhile by the 15th October the reserves had stretched their unbeaten sequence to eight games with a 3-0 win over Blackburn, Chris scoring two of them to bring his tally to 10 in eleven games and earning a headline in *The Journal* of 'Well done Waddle.'

Then after two successive defeats for the first team by Bristol City away and Swansea at home Cox decided to call up Chris Waddle and Chris Withe for the midweek game on 22nd October against Shrewsbury. Chris can still remember the excitement of being told he was playing. After all the disappointments with Newcastle the first time round, Coventry, Leeds, Barnsley and Sunderland, the months of unemployment, the years of hard slog at the factory, at last he was to pull on the famous black and white stripes at St James' Park in a Second Division Football League match. The writer was actually there that night, courtesy of a ticket arranged by Alastair Garvie, then Assistant Secretary, later to become Chris Waddle's agent, and can remember little about the match other than the weather. The whole day had been horrible and it poured with rain throughout the game which was enlivened only by a Bobby Shinton goal that was enough to get the points for United. Whilst Chris' confidence had been very high in the reserves the hustle and bustle and the pace of the League was very different. Shrewsbury made life very hard for the opposition and Chris was never relaxed.

It is perhaps worth looking at the team which played alongside Chris in his debut. There is always grim fascination about looking through old newspapers or programmes to remind oneself of yesterday's men, of forgotten heroes for it is a truism to say that old footballers never die, they simply fade away.

Kevin Carr was in goal. A lovely character much under-rated, who Chris describes as 'Mr Newcastle United.' He was always the team member who had to do presentations or meet the supporters. Arthur Cox worked him very hard, perhaps too hard, for although he overcame his weight problems he was always a bit of a worrier.

Steven Carney was at right-back, a very hard quick defender who had also been plucked from non-league football after Blyth Spartans' famous cup run. Perhaps that was why he and Chris later became close friends. Steve never gave less than 100% and was rarely taken on and beaten by pace although that wet night against Shrewsbury the crowd began to get on his back.

Chris Withe at left-back was also making his debut. He was a polite young man with a scouse accent whose ability was totally over shadowed by his older brother. He was always willing to help but his career was interrupted by a bad injury.

In the middle of the defence was Stuart Boam. Very big, very competent, always moaning about the ball being given away. Chris remembers one practice match were the reserves played the first team, when he turned to dribble past Boam. He found himself knocked to the ground and as he got up a none-too gentle tongue whispered in his ear, 'if you ever do that again you'll end up even further down.' Chris was terrified of him although later on Stuart would pick him up in the car accompanied by flasks of tea even though it was less than an hour's drive from his home in Middlesborough.

In midfield were Mick Martin, Kenny Wharton and Terry Hibbitt. Martin was a very experienced Irish Internatinal who'd played for Manchester United and West Bromwich Albion before coming to Newcastle. Off the field he was a bubbly personality but on the field he would complain all the time, although Chris realises this was probably for his own good. He was perversely nicknamed 'Zico' after the World Cup and is now a club scout.

Kenny Wharton had played in the reserves with Chris and then, as now, he gave all he got. He was very fiery for his size and would tackle anybody. On one occasion he tried to argue with Graham Roberts. Chris tried to warn him, 'don't argue with people like that.' Later in the game he trooped off past Chris for some stitches above his eye, as Chris shook his head and quietly said, 'I told you not to argue....'

Terry Hibbitt was also a complainer, making for a very noisy team. He was the most experienced man on the side but had continuing problems with his knee which eventually forced him out of the game after a short spell with Gateshead. From Terry Chris learned not to give the ball away.

Up front there was Bobby Shinton the joker of the pack who revelled in his reputation. On one occasion when walking down a shopping centre in Newcastle with him Chris saw the heads turning, the nudges, the pointing fingers – 'That's Bobby Shinton.' 'Don't you get sick of it?' Chris asked in wonder. 'Don't worry son, you'll get it in a few year's time.' Little was Shinton to realise that the sort of pressure he enjoyed was to be part of the reason for Chris' departure from his beloved North-East.

Alongside Shinton was Bill Rafferty who had scored loads of goals in the lower divisions and who scored some good ones for Newcastle before leaving in mid-season for Portsmouth. Finally Ken Mitchell, who amassed 66 appearances for the club before being released at the end of the season without ever really making any great impact.

There was nothing really special in Chris' approach to his first game. He'd taken the 59 Bus to the ground and walked in wearing the matchday suit required for all players. At the start of the season he'd not possessed such an item and had bought one for £15 in a sale. His dad and brother Joe were there as was Lorna and he came out after arranging for his guests' tickets to be asked to sign two or three autographs which he reckons to be real collector's items as they were signed in the worst handwriting ever.

After the match Arthur Cox said he had done all right but Chris knew deep down he had not done as well as he could. He also gave his first quote to the press, 'I can play a lot better than this but I never got much of the ball.' Some people might have read into that some conceit, some complaint, but in fact Chris, as ever, was simply telling it as he saw it.

Travelling home, alone and unrecognised on the bus he realised he still had a very long way to go.

# CHAPTER 15

Thursday 23rd November was a day off but the Friday found Chris on the team coach heading for the hotel in Kensington where they would stay for the away fixture with Chelsea. It was enormously exciting travelling away with the club.

Although Chris had relatives in Watford and had visited his cousin Malcolm for trips to Madame Tussauds and his Uncle Jimmy for a fishing expedition he had not been down to London for years. He'd stayed in an hotel in Spain, and a guest house when he'd seen the Manchester United and Arsenal Cup Final with the Clarke Chapman team but this was his first time in a real London hotel. He and Chris Withe sneaked out at 9.30 pm to do nothing more heinous than to buy some sweets but that was the only really sweet thing of the weekend.

Chelsea were top of the League and the crowd was nearly 23,000, almost double the gate for the match against Shrewsbury. Chris walked out to look at the pitch and found himself faced by a 'big stupid lion', the Chelsea Mascot, and the Shed baying for blood. As he went back into the dressing room and pulled on the No 9 shirt worn by such famous names as Jackie Milburn, Malcolm MacDonald and Peter Withe he felt that it wasn't going to be his afternoon. He was right. Micky Droy, the 6' 5'' giant and Gary Chivers were marking him and he didn't touch the ball more than ten times the whole match. At 4-0 to Chelsea, Arthur Cox felt the boy had seen enough and replaced him with Franz Koenen. Just before that Chris had been talking to Gary Chivers of Chelsea when Peter Rhodes-Brown raced down the left wing for the London Club with Carney and Cartwright in hot pursuit. Chris turned to Chivers admiringly and said 'he's quick' but by then Chivers too was gone and putting the ball in the net. It ended 6-0 and worse still was on 'Match of the Day' with the whole country watching it. Even Micky Droy was able to taunt debut boy Chris Waddle by pulling him into the corner, juggling with the ball and then flicking it over his enormous head.

Nobody said very much on the journey home. Arthur had said it all in the dressing room after the match. Both Waddle and Withe were dropped. Chris Waddle only thought it was the end of the world – for Chris Withe it really was and he never played for Newcastle again.

After that Chelsea debacle it was back to the reserves. It could have been worse. Less than 6,000 people saw the first team lose 2-1 at Cambridge whilst 7,000 turned up to see Newcastle's Central League team beat Liverpool for their eleventh victory in twelve games, a Liverpool side that had Steve Ogrizowicz in goal, a player who was to deny Chris Waddle his winner's medal when playing in goal for Coventry in the 1987 Cup Final. Alan Harper, Kevin Sheedy and Ronnie Whelan also played for Liverpool as did a young striker called Ian Rush. United won 2-1 and Chris scored the winner just after Rush missed an open goal (probably the last one he ever missed!).

The reserves were then jolted into a 5-2 defeat by a Coventry side that contained six of their first team. Danny Thomas did not forget to come and say hello. There was still a gulf between first team and reserve football and Chris had yet to bridge it. It's amazing how many players score feeely and perform well in reserve football but never make it at the higher level. Either they're pushed into the team too early by anxious managers looking for a lifeline to save their own jobs, or else they're kept there for too long to stop their confidence being destroyed. Arthur Cox was not such a manager and despite a terrible run by the first team that saw them lose to the likes of Cambridge and Wrexham, while scraping draws with Orient and Notts County, he still put the young players' career prospects before his own job.

Chris' first step to rehabilitation was being invited to join the squad for the Wembley six-a-side in November. Eight players squeezed into a stretch limousine. Newcastle beat Villa and Manchester City but went out to the eventual winners, Chelsea in the semi-finals with Chris scoring twice. It was looking as if the West London Club was haunting Waddle.

However, Chris did not have too long to wait before a first team recall. Ray Clarke, who'd been brought back from the likes of Bruges, Ajax and Sparta for £180,000 was sadly out of form. He'd scored but one goal, against Cardiff, in twelve appearances and indeed between November 11th and December 13th, the whole team only managed two goals, both of them scored by Bobby

Shinton. From being as high as seventh under the Cox revival they had slumped to fourteenth.

Something had to be done about goals. Arthur went out into the market and bought Mick Harford from Lincoln City. Harford was really coming home because he'd been born in Sunderland. Full of aggression on the field, he was as quiet and shy as Chris off it and on December 23rd he made his debut alongside the recalled Waddle against Grimsby Town. Chris had already played one game back in the first team against Bristol City – another goalless draw, although *The Journal* recalls, 'Chris Waddle had a first-half header saved on the line and then the youngster watched in agony in the second-half when the ball bobbled between his legs right in front of the post.' It was no Christmas treat and as one journalist said the only spectators who seemed to enjoy it were the little dancing silicon chip effigies on the new electronic scoreboard.

The Grimsby performance was little better inspite of the inclusion of Harford, who did at least hit the bar, but again the score was 0-0. Goals were becoming harder to find than new pits. Harford assumed the No 9 shirt now with Chris wearing No 11 but a 0-2 home defeat by Derby was followed by yet another 0-0 draw at Wrexham. The team had gone 450 minutes without scoring!

Christmas was strange. It was the first time Chris had been away from home over the holiday, but for professional footballers Christmas is even more a working period than usual. Although Chris was bringing home steady money his net wages were still only £50 per week so there was little over for any great luxuries. The team had to stay at an hotel for the Grimsby match on Boxing Day and left right after lunch on Christmas Day, returning to stay at another hotel in Durham for the Derby game. He felt a little lost, a little alone. The club had organised no party, although they did send each player a turkey and a bottle of sherry as a bonus. In the odd silence of an hotel at Christmas he missed his family, missed the warmth and laughter of being with his parents, his brothers, his friends, Lorna and wanted nothing more for his Christmas presents than a few goals. Probably Arthur Cox was also asking Santa for exactly the same gift. Neither of them had too long to wait.

In the first round of the cup they had been drawn at home to Sheffield Wednesday. The club was long overdue a cup run. Since the magical days of the 1950's they had suffered disappointment after disappointment, interspersed only with the occasional embarrassment such as the defeat by Hereford, the draw with Hendon or the annihilation by Liverpool at Wembly in 1974 before the watching millions. From gates of fourteen and fifteen thousand for League matches twenty-two and a half thousand people gathered at St James' Park on 3rd January 1981, such was the magic of the cup. Arthur had slotted his few signings into the team and despite the results he felt the likes of Harford, John Trewick (signed from West Bromich Albion and memorable for refusing to visit the Great Wall of China during a club tour because it was 'just another wall'), and Peter Johnson from Middlesborough formed the basis of a team that had a good chance in the cup. The whole town wanted a cup run, particularly as the League Cup's hopes had ended on away goals at Bury in August. Unfortunately Harford was cup-tied and was replaced by Ray Clarke.

The team did not disappoint their spectators this time. Chris scored both goals in a 2-1 win and Bruce Halliday, back for the first time since his nightmare Chelsea debut, was the lynchpin of the defence. Chris' first cup goal was at the Gallowgate end and after he scored he just kept running towards the supporters, fist in the air, a hundred miles high. Being a hero was a new experience. He was interviewed for local television, gave endless newspaper interviews, the press even came uninvited to his house. They were told he was visiting Ray and came round there to photograph him at his brother's kitchen sink.

Life was like that. The hero of Saturday afternoon just wanted to get back to his family. Indeed as he travelled home on the packed bus on Saturday evening after the match he could not help but listen to two supporters sitting in front of him generally moaning about the season being finished. One said to the other 'if anybody's going to turn it, it'll be Waddle.' They had no idea that the subject of their discussion was sitting right behind them. Gallowgate heroes simply didn't ride on buses like ordinary folk, they were supermen, driving their sponsored cars, sitting like Malcom MacDonald in the backs of Rolls Royces. Nothing could have been further from the truth as far as Chris was concerned.

The manager of Sheffield Wednesday that day was Jack Charlton. He always hated losing at Newcastle and the fact that this was the cup made it no easier to swallow. He was always one to find an excuse for any defeat and that occasion of his side's exit from the cup was no exception. Chris and he said nothing to each other that day; their moment was yet to come.

The headlines were all about Waddle.

'Waddle's Winners.'

'Waddle's glory ticket.'

# WADDLE

'Waddle double cheers United.'
'Waddle's Cup Wonderland.'
'Cup Crackers.'
'A Day to remember for Young Chris.'
'Sizzler from Chris.'

It was all a lot to take for the boy who had just turned twenty, who less than a year before had still been sweeping the floor and sealing up boxes at the factory. Perhaps the article that said the most was written by Colin Diball in the *Daily Mirror*. Beneath a photo of Chris and Lorna (her first exposure in the national Press) it read 'Dad cools hot-shot hero …'

'Chris Waddle won't get carried away by the two goals that shot Newcastle into today's Fourth Round FA Cup draw … his dad Joe will make sure of that.' Chris said "My dad's my biggest critic. He was at the match and he watches the reserve games to point out where I can get better. My feet are firmly on the ground." '

Everybody gathered around the radio on Monday for the Fourth Round draw. Home again, home to Second Division high flyers Luton, a team of flair and style, a team managed by none other than David Pleat. Yet again, the strands of coincidence were weaving their way through Chris Waddle's footballing career.

# CHAPTER 16

As luck would have it Newcastle's last fixture before the cup game was away to Luton. In those days they still played on grass, as Terry Venables would say, and the Geordies went down and poached a 1-0 victory through Mick Harford, long before the days he pulled on a Luton shirt.

The crowd swelled to nearly 30,000 for the return visit of Luton and apart from Shoulder replacing Wharton as substitute the team was identical to that which had defeated Sheffield Wednesday in the previous round. Again the score was 2-1 to United and although Chris didn't score he did enough to justify his place. Newcastle survived a few anxious moments, particularly when Chris gave the ball away and Ricky Hill swooped in to hit the post.

'If that had gone in I'd have strung you up,' Arthur said to Chris afterwards. Arthur was now feeling that he had got something together. He just wanted them to score goals and urged the defence and midfield to hit the ball wide to feed Harford. The moaning on the field was stopping, they were starting to believe in themselves. All of Arthur's travelling was paying off. Cox was totally obsessed with football. When he joined the club he had a brand new car which within a few months had clocked up 50,000 miles. He would go anywhere to see a player and indeed nearly bought Ally McCoist after watching him at St Johnstone. With his lads he was a real disciplinarian, the short cropped military hair making him look exactly what he was. Franz Koenen, the Dutch player was once warming up wearing a track suit bottom and Arthur chased after him, virtually having to floor him with a rugby tackle to get him to take it off.

The Fifth Round draw was not exciting. Home to Exeter. Everybody was aware of Newcastle's susceptibility to the so-called minnows, and although Newcastle was very much a slumbering giant it was still there for the killing. It was difficult to get that match out of the mind so high pitched was the local cup fever, but there was still the League and wins against Bolton and QPR did nothing to lessen confidence. Chris scored the winner against a Rangers side managed by Terry Venables, which even then played in the recognisable Venables style. It was not so much the offside game, they were just very well marshalled, always reading the game, never letting the opponents have any time on the ball. In the No 6 shirt for Rangers was Glen Roeder who would soon join Chris at Newcastle for their promotion push. Indeed it was Glen who misjudged a Bruce Halliday free kick to allow Chris to score.

January ended with the team riding high and Arthur Cox receiving the Manager of the Month award, yet there was still a slightly sour note. Chris' contract with Tow Law had ended before Newcastle signed him and so they had avoided paying any real sort of fee. The fee that Tow Law would have sought in the 1979/80 season was presumably the reason Newcastle had been 'unable to complete the deal'. Later Newcastle donated £500 to Tow Law after Chris had played nine games. The Tow Law Chairman, Harry Hodgson was not well pleased and was reported as saying 'Chris is now in the £100,000 class, yet it cost us more than £500 to develop him during the season he was with us.' He felt that Newcastle waiting to sign Chris at the end of the season was 'sharp practice', and took the size of the donation as an insult. 'If we weren't in such a bad way financially we would have sent the money back. If Newcastle United want local teams to encourage local youngsters to join them it's hardly the way to go about it.' Chris himself said nothing then, but he never forgot the churlish way Newcastle had treated Tow Law and when he had the chance to do something about it he seized the opportunity with both hands.

The home fixture with Exeter was on St Valentine's Day but the anticipated massacre just didn't happen. Thirty seven thousand people gathered for the slaughter but Exeter grabbed a 1-1 draw to take the Second Division team back to their own St James' Park. For the first time Chris flew with the team – down to the West Country. The writer arrived back from California on the morning of the game and, too tired to drive for the first and only time in his life, travelled to the match with the Supporters' Club from London. Both the trip and the match were nightmares. Stopped by the police several times on the way there the whole of the centre of Exeter was blocked off to the Newcastle supporters' transport. Exeter themselves had a pretty female physiotherapist who walked around the touchline in front of the hordes of Geordies with a bucket just before the match. Exeter won 4-0 and as one disconsolate supporter wearing his black and white scarf as a shroud said, 'Ee, after the pretty lass with the bucket it was all downhill.' Arthur Cox was even less pleased. 'You realise I'll have to dig the back garden instead of the front … when you lot go into the players' lounge, don't stand at the bar – stand in the corner.'

Once again the mid-week cameras of the BBC were there to cover the match accompanied by John Motson, who was fast becoming a bad luck symbol for the Magpies. All in all that season he commentated on their 6-0 loss at Chelsea, 4-0 at Swansea and 4-0 at Exeter!

For Newcastle the season had little more to offer, for Chris even less. On the 7th March he was substituted against West Ham and contracted a virus in the groin so serious that he could hardly walk. He stayed at home and fretted while Nigel Walker took his place; the team finally finished a respectable eleventh.

His year's contract was at an end but he was confident he'd be offered fresh terms and indeed Arthur Cox called him and said, 'you've done well. You've got the ability but you can do better.' He was to receive £120 per week basic plus £70 if he played, which was fortunate as he played in all forty-seven matches during the 1981/82 season.

Before the season started he was invited back to Bill Quay Junior Mixed Infants to present prizes and trophies at the end of the Sports' Season. His mother was now a playground supervisor at the school and that made the task no easier for him. He simply didn't know what to do or say even though only fifteen kids were present. The event goes down in posterity as his first public appearance as a football celebrity.

There were changes at the club. Willie McFaul, who had served the club as player and coach at all levels was replaced by Tommy Cavanagh as first team coach. He came from Manchester United, very ebullient in the Docherty mould. He wanted two wingers and earmarked Waddle and Walker for the roles. He also wanted 'violence' by which he meant the wingers smashing the ball hard and low across the face of the goal.

Ray Clarke had retired through injury, and Harford had left for Bristol City (en route to Birmingham via Newcastle again) to generate the money to buy Imre Varadi, the cockney with the Hungarian name from Everton.

The season started disastrously with defeats by Watford and QPR, and once again no goals scored. There was a brief revival with a 1-0 win against Cambridge but defeats by Norwich, despite a goal by Chris, saw Newcastle propping up the table yet again, as far away from promotion as ever. Arthur Cox had seen enough of the two-winger system. It may have worked for Manchester United but it certainly wasn't working on Tyneside. Then things began to look up. Varadi who'd not scored in his first seven matches got a hat trick away to Cardiff and two more at home to Derby in respective 4-0 and 3-0 wins. The fickle fans who'd begun to like Harford and who'd been getting on Varadi's back suddenly took him to their hearts; but there was still no consistency for the team lost three out of the next four matches and after an uninterrupted run of thirteen games Chris had scored only two goals, one at Stamford Bridge in yet another defeat at the hands of the London Club. The League Cup had seen another disastrous exit at Third Division Fulham.

Chris was mixing more with the other players, feeling an integral part not just of the team, but of the club itself. He and Lorna saw each other every night, argued a lot because they saw so much of each other and split up for a month. Although Chris would now go out socially with Steve Carney, Peter Haddock and Wes Saunders he never fogot his old friends. He'd see them invariably on Wednesday nights and always get them tickets for the matches. His separation from Lorna was short and temporary and soon they were back together although she was none too pleased about his punctuality. He'd arrange to meet her at 7 o'clock and often be an hour or more late when he'd been out with the lads after training. His parents were delighted by his success. Joe Senior would come to all the games and Ray who was now married would come whenever he wasn't working on a Saturday. Brother Joe, also married, mainly attended the big matches. Life was gradually changing for Chris, although he felt he was still inconsistent as a player. He had never had a formal football apprenticeship but those first two years in League football were it was far as he was concerned.

Although he was playing regularly it was a stop-start season for the team. They drew at home to Colchester in the cup, then won 4-3 away on a foggy night. Chris scored the first goal and Wes Saunders hit home a spectacular shot almost from the half-way line. It was a brief respite for in the next round they went out tamely to Grimsby. David Mills, once the most expensive player in England joined the club and added fire power up front although Varadi was scoring freely. Alan Brown also came on loan from

Sunderland and although the club wanted to buy him he failed a medical. Somehow or other Arthur Cox was determined to turn Newcastle into a scoring machine.

When they played the Orient, Frank Clarke, by now assistant manager, had the grace to come up to Chris and say he was pleased that he'd been proved wrong. Quite a few people were realising they were wrong in ignoring the talents of Chris Waddle and rumours started to abound in the newspapers of other clubs' interests in him. Terry Neill of Arsenal, Jack Charlton of Sheffield Wednesday and Allan Clarke of Leeds (who could have had him as an apprentice) were amongst the names with whom he was linked. Nobody, however, said anything directly to the player and indeed it was not until the following season that Arthur called Chris in and told him that Brighton were interested in an exchange deal for Neil McNab. Arthur offered Chris a month's loan but he declined.

By April 1983 Newcastle had sneaked up to fourth in the table and clearly had an outside chance of promotion. For Chris himself most exciting of all was his call into the England Under-21 squad for the two legged European semi-final match against Scotland. It was the first England recognition at any level for the club since Malcolm MacDonald's last cap.

Ian Butterworth of Coventry gave him a lift down after the match at Highfield Road. The training under Terry Venables and Dave Sexton was interesting and although he got no further than the substitute's bench Chris' horizons were broadening. Talking to other players, listening to men with the experience of Venables and Sexton he realised there was life outside of the North-East.

As far as life in the North-East itself was concerned he had a go at running the half marathon in the Great North Run which he thought was considerably safer than playing hockey. Lorna was carving a bit of a reputation for herself in Ladies' Hockey. Chris only went to see her play twice and on each occasion when he turned up he was told she'd already departed for hospital to have stitches in her eye and head. After that he decided he was a jinx and stayed away.

The football season itself somewhat fizzled out. Newcastle lost five of the last seven matches and finished ninth. One year of Chris' two year contract was gone. Nobody could possibly have guessed who or what the 1982/83 season held in store for the men of Newcastle United.

# CHAPTER 17

Even before the start of the 1982/83 season, Chris negotiated himself a two-year contract and scotched rumours of his departure. Again he did it himself and agreed a salary of £415 per week. It was a far cry from the dole queue but still a long way from the realisation of his true worth. The club went off on a pre-season tour of Madeira and Tommy Cavanagh called the squad together and said 'we've signed Keegan.' The squad as a man reacted with 'oh yeah.'

In fact the team came back to Keegan mania. Arthur Cox had pulled off the coup of all time. It was as if the club had won the pools. Over 2,000 would turn up to training sessions, everything was happening and when the club signed Mick Channon and then Terry McDermott and Dave McCreary to the Geordie faithful winning the League was a certainty. It was anything but that. Channon's stay was to last only a few weeks, for he just couldn't fit into the North-East, and with Keegan in the side Newcastle became the team everybody wanted to beat. A game against Keegan United was the cup final for most of the clubs in the Second Division, every young kid at Rotherham, every old pro at Cambridge wanted to be the man who dispossessed Keegan, who stopped Keegan scoring.

Keegan himself was a bonus. A very bubbly character who bought a house in Morpeth and worked his heart out both for the club and the brewery who'd effectively provided the club with the money to bring him to Newcastle. Everybody in the squad knew what he was earning because it had been so well publicised yet there was no ill-feeling. Nearly 36,000 turned out to welcome him for the first game of the season at home to QPR. Nil-nil at half-time, John Craggs hit the ball down the line, David Mills kicked it on to Kevin. Keegan didn't really connect with it that well but as it passed the goalkeeper the crowd with an enormous gulp of breath sucked it in. The writer sitting by the side of a pool on holiday in Israel

74

heard the roar on the World Service and he imagined he might have heard it even with the radio off. It was a dream start even though everybody had expected it. The rest of the season beckoned like a crock of gold at the end of the rainbow.

Newcastle beat Blackburn in the next match with Keegan scoring again but then it was back to harsh reality, defeats at Bolton and Shrewsbury, then home to Barnsley, draws in Middlesborough and Chelsea. These were not results from which championships were made and by the end of September Newcastle had sunk to twelfth position.

Things were not going too well for Chris either. He was substituted against Blackburn, which had always been a bad ground for him even when he played there for the reserves. Players do have bad grounds – once they have one or two poor performances there it gets into their minds and so much of football is in the mind. A bad player can score a hat trick against a diabolical team and then gain enough confidence to score against better class opposition. Chris lost his confidence between September and October and Arthur decided it would be a kindness to give him a rest.

Chris could not understand what was happening to him. Crowds had doubled, Newcastle were plastered over the papers nationwide, the TV cameras were always at the ground – he should have been inspired. In fact it was all too much for him. He did not talk it out with anybody, not his parents, not Lorna, not even Arthur Cox. He kept it all in his mind … and so much of football is in the mind.

When he was dropped Chris thought it was the end of the world. It was then that Brighton came in with the player exchange deal for him that he declined. He wasn't prepared to throw away all he had worked so hard for by heading for the sanctuary of the South coast. He played a few games for the reserves and then made the mistake of letting his guard drop when talking to the Press.

On 29th October 1982 the *Evening Chronicle*, under the byline of Alan Oliver, carried the headline 'Give me a new role … I'm not a winger says Waddle'. It was Oliver who had also fuelled the flame of discontent a few days before by saying that he was being watched by Birmingham, Luton, Southampton, Barnsley and Spurs.

Five minutes before a reserve match against Coventry, Willie McFaul called Chris in from the pre-match warm-up and said the manager wanted to see him. Chris raced up the tunnel.

# WADDLE

Arthur Cox went berserk. He demanded to know why Chris had been talking to the papers rather than to him and promptly fined him on the spot. Chris was back on the pitch just in time for the kick-off, and even managed to score the first goal in front of Arthur who, even at reserve matches, would sit alone in the Press Box with the window open, screaming at his players. It had been a saluatory lesson. Far too many players tell a club what they think by talking to the Press. It's an easy way of creating a transfer situation, an easy way of putting pressure on a manager and, nowadays, also an easy way to earn a bob or two.

Chris was never to do it again. If the Press have speculated about his future and career prospects then they have done so off their own back, without any help from him. His syndicated articles are carefully checked and approved and if any paper publishes anything that would bring disrepute on his club then any co-operation between that journal and Chris would soon be brought to an end.

Chris was brought back for the game against Crystal Palace in October and promptly scored the winning goal. Although Newcastle then lost to Leeds, they followed that by destroying Burnley 3-0 with Chris earning rave reviews and headlines such as – 'It's the wonder of Waddle' and 'Wizard Waddle is the Real Wrecker'.

In that match Chris scored what the papers described as the greatest goal of his career, from 35 yards. He received the ball wideish in their half and ran across the pitch, cut into the centre, beat a couple of players and hit it past an unmoving Alan Stephenson into the top corner. After that the crowd lifted him and he seemed to believe he was playing a more central striking role which was all that was needed.

Yet all the way to Christmas transfer rumours continued. He was linked in an exchange deal with Kevin Dillon of Portsmouth and Tony Henry of Bolton and indeed, without disrespect to Dillon, it's incredible to think that Birmingham actually expected Newcastle to give them Waddle and cash for him!

Len Shackleton wrote in December in *The Sunday People* 'To cash in or not to cash in? That is the question Newcastle face about wonder boy Chris Waddle.' In that article Arthur Cox said that Keegan was convinced Chris was not fit enough. 'I can understand it,' Cox confirmed, 'Waddle missed the formative years for a soccer pro between 15 and 19. Consequently he has had too much to catch up with in the professional game. He almost went to pieces at the start of the season when Kevin Keegan set Tyneside alight. Waddle just froze in the big crowd atmosphere. He's won that battle now. He is a good worker and listener in training. And he is having his best spell to-date but he has got to do the business on matchdays regularly or get out and let someone else in.'

Arthur Cox understood Chris better than he understood himself. Arthur recognised there was a battle on, a battle not just being fought on the field but inside his head. There was no way he wanted to lose the player but somehow or other he had to find a way to harness the player's talents to his real potential. He adopted a mixture of encouragement, discipline and competition. Howard Gayle, the first black player to pull on a black and white shirt had just joined the club on loan at the end of November and with Varadi and Mills there were effectively four strikers including Chris vying for two positions.

Gayle actually endeared himself to the allegedly racist Geordie fans, 'He's black he's brown he's playing for the town,' they chanted. However, after an early cup exit he was not in fact signed and when he turned up playing against Newcastle later in the season the chants changed to, 'He's brown, he's black, we sent the bugger back' – but without any real malice.

Racism amongst the players themselves is virtually non-existent and it is therefore even more disturbing that the game itself should be such a breeding ground for the scum who chant 'Monkey' at black players or worse still throw bananas. Newcastle has a more active lunatic minority than most in this respect and indeed to-date Gayle and Tony Cunningham are the only black players to appear for the Geordies. Chris has never seen racism as a problem. The well publicised rivalry between himself and John Barnes is a contest between two players. It is irrelevant that one is white and one is black. It's merely important that England has the benefit of the better of them at any one time, or indeed both of them if Bobby Robson chooses to play two wingers.

Chris had his own conflict to resolve and somehow he was distanced from what was going on about him. The Newcastle dressing room was a lively place in that 1982/83 season. It's interesting to note that in 1980/81 there was 25 matches in which Newcastle didn't score. In 1981/82, Chris' second season, it was down to 15 and in 1982/83 on only six occasions did a Newcastle side fail to hit the net. Arthur Cox that seemingly dour disciplinarian was getting together a team of entertainers, a team of flair, and with entertainment they brought character.

With the arrival of McDermott and Keegan a racing syndicate was born, then a card school again with Terry Mac and Kevin, but also with Varadi and Mills. Mick Channon in his brief stay freely gave tips in his Wurzel accent and doubtless his commuter rides with Keegan from Hampshire were filled with racing talk. On one occasion Chris was asked to go to the Doncaster sales with Mick Channon but declined saying he was not one for the horses. Indeed it was not until 1987 that the writer persuaded him to invest in a two-year-old called 'King of Knowledge' and that unfortunate animal's lack of success has convinced Chris that his own judgement was right all along.

Although the team divided itself into social groups, with John Craggs, Terry Mac and Mills as the personalities, there was no trouble-maker in that team. Craggs and Mills had been together at Middlesborough and stuck together. David Mills' career never really quite took off and his recent disasterous car accident, so nearly fatal for him, was typical of the bad luck that dogged him through his playing lifetime. 'The nearly man,' nearly a North-Eastern hero, nearly a permanent England international, it is the nearly that divides the greats from the goods in football. The local lads were also close friends by now; Chris, Steve Carney, Kevin Carr, Peter Haddock, Wes Saunders. It was not really a them and us situation but at the end of the day football is a job like every other and nobody who works in an office will wish to make close friends of everybody who works around them. Yet they are not in the public eye. The cool professional detachment displayed by some who *are* in the public eye is sometimes built up by the Press into something else, the Press who are always looking to build a mountain from a molehill.

At the end of 1982 Chris' career was really at a crossroads. He had won the November Player of the Month award in the *Evening Chronicle* but the team itself was only mid-table. No goals had come from Chris since the Burnley blinder and Arthur was still experimenting with the team. Over 30,000 supporters turned up to see Newcastle beat Derby 1-0 on Boxing Day. They were still waiting for the sleeping giant to awaken, it was just a question of how long their patience would last.

# CHAPTER 18

At the start of the 1982/3 season Chris had been promised a car if he scored 20 goals, although he says that was in fact a disincentive because it was a Skoda. He'd had some free driving lessons from Frankie Conway who had his own driving school, putting fear and trepidation into the hearts of all the working citizens of the North-East by buzzing around in a bright orange Ford Escort. The papers got hold of the story that he was driving now instead of getting a bus but unfortunately examiners must also have read the papers because it was not until his fourth test that he actually passed. Fortunately he had little time to wait between tests because he kept getting cancellations and was generally available during afternoons. Professional football has some compensations, although many players simply go to sleep in the afternoon to recover from the strain of training and as an alternative to going shopping with their wives.

'Dillon' (Alan Burdiss) was still on the dole for as he maintained there was not much demand for tram drivers. He and Chris took off for the beach at South Shields on the bus and something made them get off at a second hand car place. All of the vehicles were £300 or more except for one little old blue Capri which was marked at £100. The boys had a look at it and apart from the absence of locks on any of the doors it looked to have everything a car should have – tyres, steering wheel, engine etc. Chris bought it there and then. It was a mistake to let Dillon advise on cars. He knew nothing about them and on one occasion had given Lorna a lift home in his old Escort with strict instructions from Chris to chat her up for him. Lorna said afterwards she had not listened to a word he'd said because she was scared the car would blow up! Dillon is now in regular work, happily married and a car owner himself.

South Shields to home was only six or seven miles, but it was the first time Chris had been in a car without an instructor and by the time he set off he found himself right in the middle of the rush hour. Half way home the car ran out of petrol. After a walk to a nearby garage, the vehicle was restarted and got up to 55 mph. At that point the passenger door flew open. Chris looked at it desperately for by now he was on his own as Dillon had met a friend and decided it was wiser and safer to make his own way home. Chris drove for nearly a mile with the door swinging wildly then finally cornered and the door slammed to.

The car was not exactly Chris' pride and joy and indeed when he went to the ground for training he'd hide it in a car park. One morning he got up at home and went outside to start the vehicle. He turned the key but nothing happened and then repeated the process. After ten minutes or so the man next door who used to be a handyman came along.

'Problem?' he asked.

'Won't start,' said the non-technical Waddle.

The man lifted the bonnet.

'Shall I try and start it?' Chris asked.

'Don't bother. Someone's stolen your battery, cut the fuel pipe and drained the petrol.'

The absence of locks was obviously a bit of a disadvantage. Chris went everywhere in that first car. He was actually stopped for speeding in it and even the policeman expressed amazement that the car could do 70 mph.

Lorna also made her mark in the Capri. Chris had loaned it to her. She tried to do a U-turn outside her house. Instead of getting into reverse she'd gone into first with dire effects on a parked Vauxhall Viva. The Capri was built like a tank, the Viva was not. Chris was still asleep when Lorna in a panic came to his house and threw little stones up at the window to wake him up.

'I've crashed the car,' she said.

Chris looked at it.

'I can't see any marks on it,' he said.

'Ah, but you should see the other one,' Lorna replied.

Eventually one incident when Kevin Carr drove him back from training and the brakes nearly failed convinced Chris that he'd got his money's worth out of it and in a little dead end garage he persuaded the proprietor to allow him the £100 he'd spent on it in part exchange for a Mini.

He had the Mini for exactly one week. He went Christmas shopping with Ray and Joe Junior and parked in the ground at the Gallowgate end. When they got back it wasn't there and, convinced he'd forgotten where he'd parked it, he and his brothers traipsed all around the ground without success. Ray 'phoned the police because Chris was too upset.

On the following Wednesday Chris was out with his friends for a drink when his cousin came into the pub, told him his car had been found and offered to take him to it. When they got there it was obvious why the car could not have been brought to him. About a mile from the ground the car was skewered up high, with a concrete pillar embedded into its engine, and all of Chris' tapes missing.

With the insurance monies Chris bought a Triumph at auction. After two days the clutch went and although it was replaced the car was never the same. With Dillon in the car yet again, Chris stopped at a zebra, somebody went into the back of him and the insurance company decided it was beyond repair and wrote it off.

Nonplussed, Chris bought a Fiat. Bruce Halliday was on loan from Newcastle to Darlington and Chris and Lorna decided to go and watch him play. There was an almighty sucking noise, and Lorna looking back said, 'the window's gone,' and then had to sit all the way back on a freezing night holding a polythene cloth to keep out the elements. Shortly after that the brakes seized up and a close investigation of the vehicle found that the engine was balanced on a little bit of metal.

Tom Dolman, Chris' cousin, suggested that the time had come to buy a good decent staying car and Chris selected a Morris Marina 1300 Special which cost £1,200 from a garage in Gateshead near the Team Valley. The car looked immaculate and for a while it seemed Chris' motoring problems were at an end.

Then he was driving home across the Tyne Bridge when a blizzard blew up and he found himself driving on pure ice. In front of him was a Chinese woman driving a Fiesta. She braked and Chris, 30 yards behind also braked but nothing happened. Chris had time to tell his passenger, the young goalkeeper Paul Malcolm that they were about to crash when he saw a gap to the right of the Fiesta, steered towards it and managed to hit only its indicator. Chris' radiator went but as he topped it up with water and limped home he realised just how close he'd come to going off the bridge and into the murky waters below; but the Chris Waddle story was not meant to end there. Another year beckoned with all its challenges and, as always seemed to be the case in his life, he was to live to fight another day.

# CHAPTER 19

The third round of the cup found Newcastle paired with Brighton.
It was Chris' first trip to Brighton and the first time he'd had the
chance to see Newcastle's travelling weekend support. They
simply took over the seaside town. The writer can remember
walking along the front on Saturday morning and seeing them
coming out of their sleeping bags on the beach, exiting from
shelters or simply looking for somewhere that was prepared to
serve them breakfast. He can also remember hobbling to the
ground on a stick after a cartilage injury in a five-a-side friendly
against Arram, Berlyn, Gardner & Co – a firm of accountants who
are now Chris' financial advisers – which cut short his own
footballing career at the tender age of 37!

Brighton had a strong side although they were struggling in the
First Division and indeed ended up getting all the way to Wembley,
losing to Manchester United in a replay and then being relegated.
Now they have just gained promotion from the Third Division
while Newcastle are in the top half of the first, so speedily do clubs'
fortunes change in football.

In January 1983, however, Newcastle were the underdogs even
with Keegan, facing the likes of Grealish, Foster, Gary Stevens (later
to link up with Chris at Spurs), Peter Ward, Andy Ritchie and
Michael Robinson. Newcastle played them off the park on the day,
went one up through McDermott and then allowed Brighton to
equalise in a rare attack. The replay should have been a formality
at St James' Park. However, just as in the League Cup earlier in
the season when they'd beaten Leeds 1-0 away and then lost 4-1
at home after being one up, the occasion beat the team; the
occasion and also this time the referee.

One-nil down with twenty minutes to go Steve Carney hit home
what looked like a perfectly good equaliser. Trelford Mills, that
controversial figure disallowed it. Then just before the end the ball
went into the Brighton net again, and again the referee said no

goal. Even the Brighton players had not protested and it was hardly surprising when Trelford Mills had to have a police escort out of the ground.

Arthur Cox bought John Anderson and Steve Doyle from Preston and Anderson was now firmly a part of the team, as is still the case in 1988. Paul Ferris was not so lucky. He was fanfared all the way over from Northern Ireland and must have been something really special there. He rivalled Neil McDonald to be Newcastle's youngest ever player but never lived up to his rave reviews and eventually drifted away into non-league football, a talent that had never fully flourished.

The manager used the rest of the season to experiment and with a run of only three defeats in the last eighteen matches he seemed to be getting there. The team finished a respectable fifth and scored a total of 78 goals although Chris only scored 7. Varadi hit 22 and Keegan 21. Chris was ever present from mid-October to the end of the season and felt settled and secure enough in the North-East to decide to get married.

He and Lorna never got engaged. Chris had asked her to move in with him because he wanted to buy a house. She'd said no, so he'd no alternative but to fix the day. Neither set of parents were really surprised. Lorna's dad was a builder, and her mother ran a dry cleaners in Gateshead and together with Joe and Elizabeth Waddle they had felt for a long time that there was an inevitability about the marriage.

It was left to Lorna to do all the organising, for as the season came to an end with 30,000 faithful seeing the last home game against Sheffield Wednesday and 6,000 supporters travelling to Wolves for a meaningless 2-2 draw, the first team were off to the Far East on tour.

They flew first to Kuala Lumpur, a nightmare journey that took 30 hours. Newcastle to Heathrow, Heathrow to Rome – a two hour stop over on the plane, then on to Delhi, another wait of an hour or two, from Delhi to Abu Dhabi, then to Bangkok and finally to Kuala Lumpur.

There Montezuma's Revenge struck the whole party and they were up to little more than sitting around the pool. Big Kevin Carr was continually being propositioned by one local gay who was clearly enraptured by him. Finally Kevin could take it no longer and sounding just like Oz from Auf Wiedersehen Pet, said, 'look mate – if you don't get away I'm going to kick your balls off.' The local lad kept smiling as if this was something he would like to happen.

# WADDLE

Jet lag was another problem to contend with. Martin Thomas, signed at the end of the season from Bristol Rovers came out of the lift at 4.00 pm having just struggled out of bed after a hard night and bumped straight into Arthur Cox,

'Morning boss,' he said in a booming Welsh accent.

Eventually the team was patched up enough to play the Singapore National side and won 5-2. Steve Carney, just recovered from food poisoning after three buckets of Kentucky fried chicken, scored his first ever goal which led to great celebrations both on and off the pitch, to the bewilderment of the other spectators. The Singalese were really fast little runners – as indeed were the huge insects which lay on the pitch, moving when disturbed by the ball like something from a horror movie.

Newcastle then beat the Under-21 side and were due to play on the other side of the island. They drove through thick jungle for five hours with the bus never getting out of second gear and Chris becoming quite ill. He saw the beach with gratitude and felt that a swim might well help his recuperation. He dived in and saw everybody on the shore waving to him. He cheerfully waved back and then saw they were mouthing one word: 'sharks'. He broke every record for swimming back, the music from *Jaws* drumming in his ears. They won the match 2-0.

Chris hoped Lorna was getting on with the wedding arrangements. Newcastle's generosity did not extend to paying for any 'phone calls for the players and he was left to write letters home that might or might not arrive before he did. The team went on to Bangkok, which was an unbelievable experience. The players, with their trendy hairstyles and athletic bodies kept being touched up by local lads, who all carried handbags. Threats in Geordie did not seem to work and eventually the team kept to the hotel, rejoicing in the novelty of the floating bar with stools in the pool.

Imre Varadi was very vague. In Japan Kevin Carr called his wife very early. Imre asked where she worked and Kevin said at an estate agents. 'Ah, you're alright for cheap holidays then,' replied Imre. On another occasion Chris had seen Imre out shopping in Newcastle and next day asked him whether he'd bought anything.

'No,' he said, taking off his shirt which still had the cardboard in it!

There was a good atmosphere on that tour and indeed in the Club as a whole. Somebody found a photograph of the younger Arthur Cox and pinned it up everywhere. A nameless artist pencilled the words 'McVicar' underneath and when Arthur left

Newcastle he never forgot that. He said to Chris, 'You thought I didn't know it was you – but I did.'

There wasn't a lot about Chris Waddle, Arthur Cox didn't know by the time their relationship was at an end. They moved on to Japan where they were to compete in the Japan Cup. The film show every night in the bar was *Pearl Harbour*. Everything there was incredibly expensive. The team went to visit the golf driving ranges and discovered they would have needed a massive mortgage on their houses just to join.

The other teams in the tournament were the Japanese National Side, the Japanese National Champions, Syria (who were on stand-by to return because of the war) and Botofoga the Brazilian side. Newcastle beat Japan 4-0, the Japanese Champions 2-0 and then drew 1-1 with Syria whose equalising goal was greeted with the sort of delight reserved for the winning of the World Cup. Eventually, after a goalless draw with the Brazilian team that included Josimar and Nunez, Newcastle won the tournament on goal difference. Chris ended up the second top scorer.

When they received the award they looked at it in disbelief as it was nothing more than a big blue vase. On the trip back Keegan and McDermott got off at London and to Chris' amazement there were hordes of fans waiting to greet home their 'cup winners'. It was a testimony to the fans' loyalty, a sad statement as to how starved they had been of success and there was Chris, pushed forward to hold up his silly blue vase that was all they had to offer them. It was both funny and tragic.

# CHAPTER 20

The wedding was planned for the 25th June 1983. Chris arrived back just three weeks before to be met at the airport by Lorna who told him she'd done all there was still to do. They'd bought a house at Springwell Village before he'd gone away but Chris had seen it just the once.

Keith Mullen was to be the best man and for the stag night arranged everybody to meet at the Swan at Hewarth. There were some three dozen fellows there, all old friends, none of the players who'd all gone straight off on their own holidays after the trip. Keith had bought a bottle of Spanish Fly from a nearby sex shop. He poured most of its contents into Ray Waddle's pint of beer, and when it was time to move on Ray asked to stay on saying the beer was great.

Inevitably Gary Durham got into an argument. Ray Waddle went over to try and sort it out. A kid was claiming he was a Geordie having been born at Wallsend. Gary was querying its distance from the Tyne. The kid hit Ray on the chin and he went backwards over the table like a stuntman in a Western. He'd only intervened to say leave it, have a good night, when the kid slammed him. When Chris spoke to him the next day he told him he'd lost a tooth in a Chinese meal! The evening ended up at Tiffany's and Chris was incredibly enough still sober, although everybody who'd come to see him off was legless.

The wedding itself was very much a family affair at Christ Church, Gateshead. On the morning of the wedding, Keith Mullen came at 6 am but the cars were late. When they got to the church Keith got out and peered in through the driver's window asking 'how much is that then, two or three quid?' He'd not had a lot of experience of weddings. There was a family party at the Talk of the Tyne and Elizabeth nearly choked on a bone. Keith Mullen, as solicitous as ever said:

'Is it the pepper, Mrs Waddle?'

'No, I've got a bone stuck in my throat,' the poor woman gasped.

There was no honeymoon for they had loads to do in the house, and in any event by then the money was running low. The new 83/84 season was just around the corner and Chris really needed some bonuses. He was to get them in spades.

At the start of the season Arthur Cox had controversially sold the previous season's top scorer Imre Varadi. Imre was very popular and the crowd had no idea of the reason for the sale or of the extended negotiations that were to bring Peter Beardsley back to his native North-East. John Ryan, an Under-21 international had been acquired from Oldham to strengthen the defence and Kevin Carr seemed to have grabbed back the goalkeeper's jersey from Martin Thomas.

The first game was away to Leeds, never the easiest of places. John Anderson had scored his one goal of the season, equalling his total for the previous season, when early in the second half Kevin Carr came out for a cross and fell heavily on his elbow. Keegan offered to go in goal, but before he realised what he was doing Chris said 'I'll go in.' Arthur Cox agreed because he was scared the diminutive Keegan would be chipped. While the discussion raged everybody had forgotten about poor Carr. Chris went and pulled his shirt off and the goalkeeper screamed in agony before being carried off with a broken arm.

Within a matter of seconds Chris heard his team mates screaming 'pick it up.' He was still walking towards the goal, putting on gloves when he turned and could only see Ritchie and McClusky tearing down on him in the white of Leeds. Terry McDermott had passed back not realising Chris wasn't ready. The entire defence covered their faces but somehow or other he got the ball away. His next problem was goal kicks. All his kicks went to the left. Keegan and Mills drifted out in that direction to retrieve the ball and Chris then changed his tactics and volleyed down the middle with Keegan yelling, 'where are you going to hit it next?' Somehow or other Chris kept a clean sheet and as he ran off to leave the field a little boy came up to him and shouted,

' 'Keeper, 'keeper, you've left your goalie's bag in the net.'

When Peter Beardsley joined in October the team was 7th. He came on as a substitute in a 1-1 draw at Barnsley where Chris scored. Chris had already found the net against Oldham and Palace and was beginning to get the sort of headlines again that had earmarked his arrival in the team.

'Cracker Chris.'
'Waddle a winner.'
'Super hero Waddle.'
'Killer touch by Waddle.'
'Chris winner ...'

He was getting 9 out of 10 in newspaper ratings (which Chris himself thinks are meaningless) and after a 4-2 demolition of Portsmouth one paper said 'Move over Mac – Chris Waddle is rapidly becoming the new King of Tyneside.' No less a critic than Jackie Milburn used epithets like 'wonder', 'magical', and 'masterpiece' in a review of Chris's performance that day.

Arthur Cox talking to the press expressed his disappointment that John Ryan was in the Under-21 side while Chris was temporarily out of favour. He said: 'Indeed the way he's playing now I would put him infront of John Barnes who could well be in the full England side. Certainly Waddle is more talented than Barnes but he lacks the Watford player's consistency; but having said that I doubt if there is a more exciting player than Waddle in the country at present. He is so talented but in the past he has lacked the confidence to take advantage of it.'

Whether it was his marriage, or the arrival of Beardsley, or simply the fact that goals breed confidence – and probably a combination of all three – there was no doubt that in the autumn of 1983 Chris Waddle was a player on the very top of his form. He was more settled, more responsible. He enjoyed being a house owner, paying a mortgage, buying furniture and decorating. He looked forward to going home every night and telling Lorna what had gone on during the day. He was happy to get up at 7 am even when he didn't need to, just to drop Lorna off. Success on the field in no way changed him. He still kept to his old friends and around this time he got close to Stephen Preston, who worked with Lorna and was later to be responsible for marketing many Waddle souvenirs.

It was Stephen Preston who got Chris to take on his first management role in running 'The Azure Blue' pub side. They were mainly single lads bereft of the niceties of an organised club – if someone hurt his leg then he had to have orange-juice put on it because they had no sponge. They trained on Wednesday night at Newcastle's gym but Chris would rather have had them play their matches on a mid-week than on Sunday. Their Saturday night drinking excesses meant they propped up the league for most of the season.

Chris would give them circuits and bunny hop training on Wednesday and by the matches on Sunday many of them could still hardly walk. They actually got to the semi-finals of the cup and Chris, hoping to inspire them, told them to really fight. In fact they were 3-0 down after 10 minutes which was typical of their performances which led to his frustration. Steve Preston was a good secretary and treasurer but was somewhat lacking in footballing ability. If Chris played him and he scored everybody would have to listen to him talking them through it for at least a month afterwards. The team's centre-half was a massive lad called Ian Elliot with a huge square head in the Herman Munster mould. He had no fear whatsoever and would slide tackle on really hard surfaces his skin rolling up like the lid of a sardine tin. His legs were tree trunks marked by varicose veins and Chris would just give him the job of man-to-man marking the opposition's best player. There was nothing subtle about the team but it kept Chris firmly in touch with his own roots.

Arthur Cox was also working hard at keeping the lad's feet on the ground. He was actually substituted after scoring twice against Portsmouth because Arthur didn't think he was looking hungry enough for a hat trick. Again the team had a rapid exit from the Milk Cup drawing at home to Oxford and losing 2-1 away despite a Keegan goal, despite hordes of visiting supporters (including the writer) and despite Oxford having a man sent off. Keegan could not yet walk on water despite what 30,000 Geordies believed.

Charlton, Swansea and Cardiff were all demolished and that brought Newcastle into second place, although left with a match at home to the other promotion favourites Manchester City. Everybody felt it was going to be something special including the writer, who decided to take his family up to the North-East for the weekend to stay at the County Hotel which also housed Peter Beardsley and his wife and poor Malcolm Brown. Malcolm had joined from Huddersfield only to suffer a serious injury in training and than aggravate it by slipping on the hotel bathroom floor!

Newcastle were irresistible that day, a definitive performance in front of over 33,000 people – an incredible crowd for a Second Division match. They would have beaten anybody. Poor Williams, the black Manchester City goalkeeper had to suffer the usual racial abuse and five goals put past him; one from Keegan, one from Chris and a hat trick from Beardsley. Seven-year-old Nicky Stein decided to get Beardsley's autograph on Sunday morning. Ignoring the 'Do not Disturb' sign on the player's door at 9 am he knocked, and knocked, until he did finally capture his signature for his book.

Yet afterwards it looked for a while as if the bubble had burst. They struggled to beat Fulham 3-2, then had yet another unhappy visit to Stamford Bridge where Chelsea beat them 4-0. Four more were put past them at Hillsborough by Sheffield Wednesday and although they beat Cambridge 2-1 through a Keegan penalty they then lost 3-2 to Derby after being 2-0 up at half-time. Arthur Cox missed seeing the team he was to manage as he had an ear infection, and indeed quite a few of the Newcastle team had earache as well after Keegan had raved and ranted at them in the dressing room for throwing it away.

Derby had pressured them all the time and it was looking as if all a team had to do away from St James' Park was to put the pressure on and Newcastle would simply crumble. Chris thinks that may even explain their cup record as lower division teams who batter away will believe in themselves enough to get a result.

In December the *Evening Chronicle* contained a report of a Birmingham bid for Chris but nothing came of it. Nothing came of Chris' hopes to get back into the national Under-21 side either. Tommy Cavanagh had given some good reports but to no avail and Chris thought that perhaps he'd been put in the team too early.

Then they seemed to get back on a run again with a 5-2 drubbing of Huddersfield and a 1-0 win at Brighton, Chris scoring twice in the first of these and the winner in the latter. They brought his tally to eight goals, as many as he'd scored in the whole of the previous season. He was revelling in the freedom given to him by Arthur Cox and triggered off by playing alongside McDermott, Keegan and Beardsley. Then Newcastle heard the draw for the third round of the FA Cup – they were away to Liverpool.

# CHAPTER 21

Fame was beginning to demand a price. On one occasion Chris was hanging around the City centre with Wes Saunders and Micky Sloan when they decided to have a drink. A lad in the bar was moving stools around when he suddenly said to Wes that he intended wrapping one around his neck. Wes' response was, 'you would, would you?' and the next thing Chris knew was that Wes and the lad were rolling about on the floor. The publican asked them to leave which they promptly did and went on to the next pub. As they were walking along a police car pulled up alongside. 'Are you Wes Saunders?'

'Yes,' and with that he was bundled away to Chris' horror and astonishment. In fact no charges were ever levelled and although Arthur Cox summoned the players in he accepted their explanation. It's a problem of being a footballer – or indeed anybody in the public limelight; if you go out socially you run the risk of being threatened. Years later a Sunday newspaper latched on to the story and suggested that it was only Chris' marriage to Lorna that had saved him from becoming an aggressive alcoholic; but by then Chris had learned to rise above such rubbish, for there seemed no depth to which the gutter press would not stoop to fabricate a story.

Terry Sprott was at the centre of another incident. A game was off and Chris, Terry and some other friends went to their local to celebrate Terry's birthday. Terry managed accidentally to spill drink over the local darts team. Somebody then came over and said to Chris that he was responsible as it was one of his mates. They then got very aggressive and aimed a punch at him, the police were called and the drunken lad then ran outside shouting, 'it's Chris Waddle, it's Chris Waddle.'

Fortunately Chris had many witnesses to say he had done nothing, and indeed anybody who knew him would testify that he is the last person to get mixed up in a fracas. Be that as it may he had to face up to Arthur Cox yet again and this time he fined the player just for being there.

There's no real answer to it. What does a player do? Not go out? Even in London where the Waddles have found a privacy that was never available to them in the North-East, kids will still pass him in the street chanting, 'Gunners, Gunners.' They can then go to work next day and claim that they wound up Chris Waddle. Chris' attitude now is that if it makes their day, it doesn't hurt him and he'll let them enjoy it. The important thing is not to bite on the line they cast into the water – once you do that then they've won.

Back in 1984 Chris still had something to learn about his relationship with the public, but on the field things were going well. He hit the winner with the outside of his left foot from the edge of the box at the Gallowgate end, in front of nearly 30,000 of the faithful. A goal described by Ronnie Galvin of Barnsley as 'sheer magic, really world class.' Indeed most of that crowd seemed to be at Anfield the following Friday night when, although the team lost on the pitch, the fans completely outsang the Kop.

The match was televised and almost inevitably Newcastle froze. Although Liverpool were a yard quicker, United never really did themselves justice. Chris had probably the best chance of the night but Grobelaar saved it and once again there was an early exit from the cup, this time 4-0.

The match was not merely a lesson for Chris and the other young players but also for the more experienced Keegan. On one occasion Chris knocked the ball down to Kevin who had 5 yards start on Mark Lawrenson and lost it. Never one to do anything unless he could do it perfectly Kevin realised he could no longer compete with the very best in the game and announced that whether or not Newcastle were promoted, he would retire at the end of the season. There is no doubt in Chris' mind that Kevin could have played on for a year or two, moulding the young team together; but Kevin had worked hard during his career and there are not that many players who have sufficient pride in their performances, or indeed sufficient cash behind them, to say at 33 that enough is enough.

Everybody was shocked by the announcement including Arthur Cox. The First Division beckoned with Newcastle nicely positioned in fourth place and perhaps it was Keegan's decision more than anything else, the fact that Arthur would only have Keegan, Beardsley and Waddle together for one season that drove him and the side so single mindedly towards promotion. Looking back

Arthur had assembled an incredible team for the Second Division, for in addition to the trio of goal scorers, he had John Anderson, David McCreary, both internationals, one for Eire and one for Northern Ireland, Glen Roeder, joined just before Christmas, a central defender who had just missed out on deserved internatinal honours, and the undoubted emerging talents of Neil MacDonald who was to play for the England Under-21's. If Newcastle were ever going to escape from the lower divisions it had to be now. Chris acknowledges that that side contained the best front three he has ever played with.

A bad winter held them up and they were reduced to road running or just kicking around in the snow. Obviously players always prefer to play rather than train. When Newcastle finally got back on the road at the end of January there was no win bonus anyway because they lost 3-1 at Palace and although they beat Portsmouth 4-1 away (finally winning in a televised match against a side that contained the young Mark Hateley who was later to become Chris' England room mate) they then lost at home to Grimsby, of all teams, slipping to fifth in the League.

They went to Maine Road to face Manchester City again in a crucial match on February 18th. Some 12,000 supporters travelled down that day to swell the crowd to 41,767 and they were not disappointed. Goals by Beardsley and Keegan saw them 2-0 up at half-time and although City pulled one back the incredible support from the terraces inspired Newcastle to hold on. Wherever Chris has gone, wherever he may go in his career he cannot believe that anything will better the support Tyneside gives to Newcastle United. Even without success they turn up in droves. Men who have supported the club since childhood still stand on the terraces singing, *Blaydon Races* when the side is winning or *We'll support you evermore* when they're 4-0 down. They never give up hope, never believe a game is lost – or indeed won, and indeed with Newcastle's history of total unpredictability who can blame them?

Yet after the Grimsby defeat the team got a grip on themselves. Chris won the *Evening Chronicle* Hennessey Cognac Player of the Month award for January and was turning on the sort of performances that were attracting the attention not just of other clubs, but also England Manager, Bobby Robson.

They beat Cardiff, with Chris scoring again, then put together an unbeaten run of another seven games with wins against Middlesborough, Swansea, Leeds and Charlton and draws with Fulham, Chelsea and Shrewsbury. By the time they met Sheffied

# WADDLE

Wednesday in mid April they were back up in the top three, and instead of singing Chris' virtues the newspapers were carrying headlines like 'Waddle Wanted – Man United trail Newcastle Striker' and 'Hands-off Waddle'. Stan Seymour – Mr Newcastle – the Club Chairman was moved to say:

'There is no way Chris will be allowed to leave this club. We have him under contract until the end of next season and we expect him to be a Newcastle player beyond that.' Expectation was one thing, fact another.

Although Chris knew Manchester United were watching Newcastle's game he had no idea as to whether or not they were watching him in particular. Transfer rumours are started in odd ways. The newspapers look at a likely target, see how long he's got to go on a contract and if it's a short period there's a kernel of a story. They then watch to see which managers or scouts are in the crowd and put two and two together often coming up with five.

In the 87/88 season Chris has been linked with Everton and Man United, plus French and Italian clubs, players like Nigel Clough have been associated with Liverpool, Man United, Spurs and Italy, Paul Gascoigne with Man United, Arsenal, Spurs and Liverpool. It's a bit like a racing tipster naming every horse in the race in his article – he can always pick out the relevant bit the next day and say he tipped the winner. For the most part though it's all guesswork, but guesswork that can cause an enormous amount of damage to the relationship between the player and the club. The player becomes unsettled and, even if he had no idea of leaving, the newspapers sow the seeds in his mind and as far as the club is concerned they're often convinced their player has been 'tapped up' ie illegally approached. During a player's contract no other team can approach him except through his club, who can agree or not as they choose for him to be spoken to. Often the easiest approach is through the newspapers. A word to a journalist by an interested club that they're eyeing a player – the article appears and the effect is the same. Football, like every other business, has it seamier side.

After a draw at Blackburn and a 5-1 drubbing of Carlisle, Newcastle travelled to lowly Cambridge needing to win to be sure of promotion. Cambridge had gone some twenty matches without a win and were heading for a dubious club record in that respect. It was an all-ticket match and again thousands made the long trip to greet their heroes. It was not to be. It was a disaster from the start. The club took the wrong shorts and had to borrow a set from

94

Cambridge. Thus indebted to the opposition they paid them in full by allowing them to win 1-0. The news came through that their promotion rivals Grimsby had drawn and as the players trooped disconsolately off the pitch a supporter ran up the tunnel and into the changing room – only to be thrown out by Arthur and Ken Liversedge. 'Blew it again you stupid bastards.' There was no blaming him, nor could the team object to the car loads of supporters who overtook the team coach on the way back giving 'V' signs.

There were three games left, home to Derby and Brighton and away to Huddersfield. There was no margin for error.

# CHAPTER 22

Bank Holiday Monday – 5th May 1984 – saw 35,866 people pack into St James' Park for the visit of Derby. For once everything went right. Two-nil up at half-time with Chris and Peter Beardsley scoring, then in the second half Beardsley scored again and the inevitable Keegan goal made it 4-0. Newcastle were back where they belonged in the First Division, and it was the first success Chris had really experienced at professional level. There were the inevitable laps of honour, the constant chanting of the heroes names, the champagne in the dressing room but afterwards there was a bit of an anti-climax. Newcastle laid on nothing for the players nor their wives and everybody was just left to make their own way home. Chris went out to the local with Lorna that evening and on looking back realises that he could have enjoyed it so much more if the club themselves had made it more of an occasion. It is hard to pinpoint precisely when the disillusionment with Newcastle as a club first set in, but that night is as good a place as any.

The supporters, however, were still on a high. Thousands flocked to a mid-week draw at Huddersfield and then the biggest home gate of the season assembled for Keegan's farewell against Brighton. Chris scored one, Beardsley another and then, just as he had scored in his first game against QPR, the little man knew his lines well enough to score for the occasion, from a rebound. The crowd went mad. They kept singing and singing and after Chris and the rest of the team had done their fifth or sixth lap of honour they left the stage to Keegan.

Kevin had played his last match for United, but Chris was about to step out into pastures new, to compete with the best in the world's most competitive League; the English First Division.

Looking back on that promotion year Chris realises now that it was all part of the learning process. He can watch and re-watch videos and know that some of the mistakes he made then he could

On the run against Leicester

*Photo: Action Images*

Dream debut — Chris celebrates the first of his two goals in his opening match for Tottenham against Watford, August 1985          *Photo: Syndication International*

Waddle beats Sansom to the ball in the North London derby of February 1987
*Photo: Action Images*

Scoring the only goal of the match against Liverpool, March 1987

Photo: David Cannon/Allsport

Celebrating that same goal (Gary Stevens left, Glenn Hoddle right)

*Photo: Press Association Photos*

Slicing through the Milan defence in Ardiles' testimonial, May 1986

Photo: Action Images

A change of role for Chris as he takes to the microphone for his record with
Glenn Hoddle

Scoring against his old club: Tottenham v. Newcastle, August 1987

*Photo: Action Images*

not make now. In 1988 there is not so much of the analysis – more an immediate awareness of errors on the field, which then have to be expunged from the mind at once in order to get on with the game, to concentrate on what happens next, rather than what has just occurred. He is no great analyser of the opposition, and will listen politely and patiently to managerial or coaching pre-match talks, but has sufficient confidence in his own abilities to know that if his game is right then on the day he can beat anybody.

In that spring of 1984 the Newcastle team had taken a giant step forward. They were the lucky ones. Chris particularly singles out Ronnie Glavin of Barnsley as a player who could have bridged the gap between Second and First Division football, yet he was not to be so lucky, he would never have the chance. Curiously he was one of the players linked time and time again with Newcastle, even once in a part exchange deal with Chris. Who knows how many Glavins there are today outside the First Division, even in non-league football just waiting for the chance, players who have missed the nets trawled by the premier clubs. Vinny Jones of Wimbledon was after all a Willesden player less than two years before he won his Cup Final medal.

Kevin Keegan had certainly not missed out on the big time. On the Thursday night after the end of the season 38,000 were there to see a friendly against Liverpool, which was partly to raise money to buy new players. It was a night of drama and emotion, although for once Kevin didn't score on cue – Terry McDermott his long time friend and henchman netted Newcastle's two. At the end on a freezing cold night a helicopter landed on the pitch and whisked Kevin a mile or so up the road to a reception at the Gosforth Park Hotel. The rest of the team simply collected their cars and went up to join in the celebration.

Considering the job the players had achieved on the field the club was hardly effusive in its thanks. There was no organised tour, not even a few days holiday. Chris and Lorna went off to Cyprus and while he was away Newcastle showed their gratitude to the manager and their ongoing confidence in him by offering a short contract. Arthur Cox perceived it to be the insult that it was and resigned. By the time Chris got back he was gone and he learned through the papers that he'd immediately been snapped up by Derby County, in the confidence that he would achieve for the Peak District what he had done for Tyneside.

Still on holiday Chris bought an English paper. The news was less than encouraging. Newcastle had appointed Jack Charlton.

# WADDLE

Chris could only think of Middlesborough and Sheffield Wednesday and neither thought was very exciting. Both had been better known for their work rate than identity, neither team had been allowed to operate a star system. Yet, Chris was not the sort of person to dismiss anybody without giving them a chance. He'd been dismissed himself too often. He had a year left of his contract and was dying to play in the First Division. If anybody had asked him if he wanted to leave Newcastle United he would have thought they were joking. Disillusion was soon to set in.

Jack Charlton's arrival at St James' Park was less than subtle. He looked at everybody, pointed at David McCreary and said 'introduce yourselves.' It was quite clear he knew nobody and had not bothered to familiarise himself with names beforehand either. Some may call this plain indifference, others eccentricity.

Terry McDermott was the first to fall out with the new manager. His contract was up and he was entitled to a free transfer. He was one of the players involved in a five-a-side game when big Jack came up and told them all to stop.

'I don't want you playing one-two's on goal. I want you to play one-two's with God.'

The players looked at him mystified. He re-started the session with two players standing at the end of the gym on benches and the rest being told to chip the ball into their hands.

'That's what I mean by one-two's with God. You can't be hurt as long as the ball is up in the clouds.' It was a dubious philosophy to try to impose on a team which had shown considerable flare in scoring eighty-seven times the previous season. Chris felt it simply took the skill out of that element of training.

With Keegan gone, Glen Roeder took over the captaincy. He was a popular choice, and even more popular was the reappointment of Willie McFaul to first team coach. Willie took the pre-season training and had the squad running out of the Benwell gates for the six or seven miles to Hexham. Charlton came to watch and picked on Steve Carney and said, 'he's the pacemaker. Follow him.' It was an unlikely choice, for however quick Carney was on the field he was no long distance runner. Steve plodded along for a while and then everybody got bored and kicked on past him. Chris and Steve trailed in so distantly last that everybody was changed. Charlton was not impressed.

'Right, it's a lap of Benwell you two.' He then grabbed a kid's bike and cycled round the circuit encouraging them, a huge almost comical figure wearing his inevitable cap.

The pre-season matches were up in Scotland. The team's defenders had been working on such useful talents as flicking the ball on to one foot and volleying it. He had toyed with a sweeper system and rejected it. The players were unhappy and it showed in a poor performance against Morton, although they won 2-0, a 0-0 draw with Kilmarnock and a 1-0 victory at Partick. Willie McFaul was in charge for the last game against Hibernian. The team ignored everything Charlton had told them, went out and played football as they were accustomed to and won 5-1. The first hour was the best that Chris remembers Newcastle ever playing, even better than their destruction of Manchester City in the promotion year.

All the pre-season friendlies proved was that Jack Charlton's methods did not seem to be working; but the team had yet to play its first match back in the big time. That was on 25th August 1984, away to Leicester. It was the fastest game Chris had ever played in. Steve Carney scored, then McCreary and Chris got the winner. Afterwards he was hot and absolutely exhausted, but it was worth it to kick the campaign off with a win.

Nearly 30,000 came to St. James' at the height of the holiday season and saw United win 2-1 against Sheffield Wednesday who'd come up as champions the previous season. Everybody was tired and stiff but meanwhile it was six points out of six. Jack Charlton was keeping his distance. He had a lot of previous engagements and wanted to see them through, and day-to-day control was with Willie McFaul. Yet it was Jack who suggested Chris play up front right from the pre-season friendlies, and there was no doubt he was much happier there.

Then, on the eve of the home match against Aston Villa tragedy struck the Waddle household. Chris was woken by an early morning call from his brother, Ray, 'I didn't want to ring you because I knew you had a game, but we felt you ought to know that Dad's had a stroke.'

Joe Senior had been pushing himself very hard. Just three months before, he and Elizabeth had split up. Although he was retired he still loved to go dancing and live his social life at a frantic pace. Something had to give and eventually it did. Some five or six years before he'd had pleurisy and by the time he had his first stroke he was 70. Before his illness he had looked a fit 50, but when Chris saw him he was very shocked. His speech was affected and overnight he'd turned into an old man. It was Chris' first encounter with serious illness. He returned to the first team, scored and typically said nothing. Instead Newcastle played Villa off the park. Chris scored twice, both for his Father and earned himself a headline in the *Sunday Sun* of 'Magic Man.'

The reporter wrote:

'Anyone who has doubts that Waddle is a genuine contender for an England Cap should just ask Aston Villa's defenders.' Even Jack Charlton was as near euphoric as Chris ever saw him. 'Waddle saves his energy and then explodes. When he does he's terrific.'

Peter Beardsley added a tribute to his front-running partner:

'No one in the world would have stopped Chris today. Those goals were magnificent.'

With nine points out of nine the newly promoted Newcastle United were top of the First Division. Chris still has the cutting of the League Table in his scrapbook. It looked as if the glory days had returned to Tyneside.

# CHAPTER 23

United went to Highbury on 4th September full of confidence, heads held high. Ninety minutes later they left with their tails between their legs. Chris believes that if Carney had not got himself booked for an early tackle on Charlie Nicholas it might have been different, that his restraint in fear of a second booking and dismissal took the bite out of the side, but most spectators saw it as men against boys. Although Newcastle were only beaten 2-0, it could have been much worse than that.

In the first three games of the season they had taken everybody by surprise. First Division defences were not familiar with Peter Beardsley and Charlton devised a fairly basic tactic of long balls played through for Beardsley and Waddle to chase; provided they beat the off-side trap it was one-on-one and Charlton quite rightly fancied his men's chances. Gradually teams recognised the tactic and refused to let Chris or Peter get in behind them. Chris now believes the manager could have been more flexible and adapted the system, but he wouldn't. The whole team thought he was wrong but he either did not agree or else refused to admit it. He was the manager and they were only players.

Glen Roeder with all his experience had tried on one occasion to slow things down by putting his foot on the ball but Charlton gave him a roasting.

'I never want to see you do that again – you could slip.'

Newcastle slipped to a 5-0 defeat at Man United and then lost 2-3 at home to Everton, dropping from top to tenth in the League. The honeymoon was over, the message finally got through to Big Jack. During the week before that QPR match he took the team to Gateshead Stadium where there was a new astroturf pitch in order to try to get them acclimatised to QPR's artificial surface. He also changed the system and decided to play Chris up front, with Beardsley just behind him coming out of midfield. He knew QPR would try and play an offside trap and the instruction to Kevin Carr in goal was to get the ball to the full-backs. Thereafter Malcolm Brown would hit the left-wing, Wes Saunders the right. It worked like a dream. By half-time United were 4-0 up. Yet in the dressing room their manager was not convinced. He told them to keep going, to do exactly what they'd done, but his hesitation got through to the side. QPR pushed Terry Fenwick into midfield and rapidly pulled back to 4-3. Then Newcastle got another and at 5-3 with two minutes to go felt the three points were theirs. It was not to be, Rangers scored twice in a match that could have finished 10-10, but which ended 5-5.

In the dressing room Chris disappeared rapidly into the showers. With a hat-trick under his belt he thought he'd be free from criticism. He was right. But Charlton did go crazy. In all his career in football Chris had never seen anything like it. He was swearing and ranting and looked close to hitting somebody. On the coach going back he went up to every individual and when he got to Peter Haddock, said, 'I saw you in the last twenty minutes bent up saying I'm f.....d.' Chris did remember the match ball, but only just, and could hardly blame Jack for his reaction.

They had conceded 15 goals in four matches and were always struggling against set pieces. Anything that went into the box spelled trouble. Charlton told Kevin Carr, the 'keeper, 'go for everything in the box,' but Kevin was not a Bruce Grobelaar and the advice and its effect shattered his confidence. Jack, however, did not worry unduly about players' feelings or sensitivities.

It was all down to inexperience. Any team with a few old heads in it would have calmed it down and held on against QPR, but Glen Roeder, who had a long career behind him, had spent most of it in the lower divisions and there was nobody with big time experience behind them. Chris now thinks Jack should have bought, there was no doubt of that but instead he waited until the rot set in and then went for Pat Heard, Tony Cunningham and Gary Megson – all ex-Sheffield Wednesday.

Heard was the first. Nobody knew anything about him and he arrived in exchange for John Ryan, who'd never really settled. Chris had played against Ryan at Oldham and had been really impressed. Obviously the England selectors had been too because he'd been drafted into the Under-21 squad; but at Newcastle playing before crowds of nearly 30,000 was a vastly different prospect to the empty spaces that contained only 6,000 and his career never really developed. Sometimes it happens and in fact for Ryan it was downhill all the way after his departure from the North-East, a prospect who never really fulfilled his potential.

After the QPR debacle the inclusion of Heard gave some balance to the midfield and they began to string together a few results with an unbeaten sequence of seven matches, although only Ipswich and Chelsea were beaten. Chris scored in both victories bringing his goal tally to nine by November and rumours abounded about his imminent selection for the Under-21 squad. Jack Charlton was not enthused. In *The Star* of the 3rd September he was reported as saying 'I don't want him to play for England just yet.' He gave no reason and fortunately the England selectors took no heed. In October Chris was called up as the over-age player in the squad against Finland, just four years after leaving Tow Law. Chris was pleased for himself but even more delighted for Joe Senior who was still in hospital recovering from his stroke. He still has that formal letter today.

Two days after he received that invitation Chris scored the goal against Bradford City that saw Newcastle pass the second round of the Milk Cup for the first time in eight years. The head lines kept rolling in, 'Top Chris,' 'Waddle is your man Bobby' and somewhat disturbingly, 'Pay up or I go,' an opening to an article in the *Sun* when he won the *Sun* Canon Player of the Month award. He wasn't money grabbing, but his contract was up at the end of the season. He was listening and he was learning, hearing what others were paid, realising what he was worth. Newcastle had to realise it too and recognise his desire for security. Apart from the deal with Keegan, where his salary had been topped up by the sponsors, Newcastle were not noted for being the best of payers. They kept their wages bill down by signing hard-working players rather than stars and Charlton treated the club's purse as if it were his own. Apart from that their bonus scheme was one of the worst in the League – cumulative bonuses developing from £120 by £20 a match won then going back to the original £120 if there was a defeat or a loss. This meant that it was almost impossible to reach the top level of the bonuses and if the club won five consecutive matches and then drew away with Liverpool they would still be back to square one. The deal was only altered at the end of the 1987/88 season when the club was faced with a players' revolution and finally installed a more realistic system.

On the 24th October Bobby Robson came to watch Chris at St James' Park in a 1-1 draw against Forest. Shortly afterwards Jackie Milburn, for so long a devoted fan of Waddle's talents, wrote an open letter to the England manager in his newspaper column headed 'Waddle is your man Bobby.'

'Surely his England chance cannot long be delayed,' he ended, yet when the full England Squad was announced for the World Cup clash in Turkey the name 'Waddle' was not amongst the 23 selected. But there was still plenty of time. He duly made his debut against Finland for the Under-21's and scored in the second minute with the team going on to win 2-0 and Chris making the second. *The Journal*, not known for its impartiality, described him as the 'Man with the deadly finish.'

He played up front, where he liked to be in the first-half and in the second-half on the left-wing, but wherever he played he was just thrilled to be selected. It was the first time he met with other players away from the club atmosphere. There was Nick Pickering, Barry Venison, who was to end up at Liverpool, Paul Parker, then with Fulham now freely tipped for full honours with QPR and Trevor Steven who has so often played alongside Chris in the full England team. Everybody else was a regular, everybody else knew each other, yet Chris was welcomed into the fold and in no way made to feel the poor relation.

He returned home full of it, yet on the Sunday after the Liverpool game beckoned, a game that would really see if Newcastle had learned any lessons, a game that was to be televised into the homes of millions.

# CHAPTER 24

Everybody in the club knew that if Liverpool were to be beaten, if the memory of the 4-0 drubbing was to be erased then Newcastle had to be ahead at half-time. Liverpool, then as today, had a reputation of growing stronger and stronger as the game proceeded and if they had an Achilles heel it was to give a team a chance to get an early goal. Newcastle had that chance and it fell to Chris Waddle. He was put clear through and then his right foot slid on the wet surface and across. He had one more chance but was flattened by the advancing Grobelaar and shot over the bar. Newcastle tried hard, but they tired and two goals by Liverpool saw them home. It was back to the drawing board yet again, one step forward, two steps back. The defeat pushed the team down to fourteenth, the lowest they had been all season.

This stage of the season was disastrous all round for Chris. He'd picked up an injury against Chelsea and had had to pull out of the Under-21 team to go to Turkey. In fact as things turned out if he'd gone he would have got into an injury-stricken side. Perhaps the time wasn't quite right, for fate has always finally been on Chris' side.

December brought a home defeat to Southampton and then a 2-1 win at home to Stoke with Chris scoring yet another goal to add to his Milk Cup effort against Ipswich which was not enough to keep Newcastle in the competition. It also brought an away game against Tottenham Hotspur which was to prove the match that changed his life, although he did not know it himself until many months later.

What he did know was that Spurs were the kind of team to give the opposition a chance to play. In fact Newcastle had innumerable chances in the first half, one of which they were convinced was over the line. Then in the second half Beardsley chipped the ball over, Chris brought it down in the box, body swerved Paul Miller and hit it into the net. It was a goal of perfection, a goal shown over and over again on television, a goal that made Tottenham determined to make Chris Waddle their player.

The result was in a way an irrelevance. Spurs were given a disputed penalty, when Wes Saunders was supposed to have brought down John Chiedoze and then scored twice more, once again demonstrating Newcastle's lack of experience. The papers were all raving about Chris. Peter Shreeve, the Spurs manager said; 'Some of the things he did were world class. He always frightened me when he had the ball.' Bobby Robson was there and told the Press afterwards, 'He makes some tremendous runs and gets behind people – and he scored a hell of a goal. He has a great touch.'

'World Class Waddle' screamed the *Sunday People*.

'World Class' echoed the *News of the World*.

A week later Chris scored against Norwich in an otherwise uneventful 1-1 draw. He had 14 goals now, almost as many as he'd scored in the whole of the previous season in the Second Division. The world seemed to be at his feet. Even Jack Charlton was prepared for his England call up. 'Chris will be part of the England set-up before the summer. I know Bobby Robson likes him … Chris is ready.'

Although Chris' dad was stable he was not getting better. His left side was paralysed and whilst he could read what was going on in the papers his days of going to St James' Park with his boys seemed to be at an end. What he read of Chris was encouraging; the results of the team, less so.

They lost 4-0 at Villa, 2-1 to West Bromwich Albion and 3-1 to Arsenal at Christmas. Chris was still playing up front but, with the arrival of the aggressive Ian Baird on loan he was moved to the left-wing. Jack Charlton thought the team was too lightweight in attack. He took Ian Baird on because he wanted somebody to get into people. Baird certainly did that. He played five times, was booked on almost every occasion and was sent off in a reserve match!

Notwithstanding the miserable series of results over 36,000 people came to St James' Park on New Year's Day and again in late 1985 for the first derby match against Sunderland since 1979/80 season. Chris had hurt his knee and was forced to watch the match from the stands but he and the partisan crowd saw a pulsating thriller from start to finish. Newcastle won 3-1, Beardsley got a magnificent hat-trick and after a series of bets being taken in the stands as to whether Wes Saunders or Howard Gayle (by now a Sunderland player) would get sent off: it was Gayle who got his marching orders. By now Chris had buried all his childhood support for Sunderland. It was difficult to forget they had turned him down, but even then he did not want them to be relegated – he looked forward to the Tyneside-Weirside battles far too much. Newcastle could have won by five and it was understandable (although mystifying to opposition supporters) that for years afterwards the Geordie faithful would sing *A man shall live for evermore because of New Year's Day*.

There was still no cup glory for Newcastle though. They led against Forest away through a Gary Megson goal but were pegged back by a thunderbolt from a certain Johnny Metgod who teamed up with Chris at White Hart Lane in 1987. At home in the replay Chris scored and had three cleared off the line. Again Forest equalised, the match went to extra time and Newcastle duly bowed out 1-3. It was beginning to occur to Chris that Newcastle was very far from a side that was going to compete for honours, just as it had dawned on Malcolm MacDonald and was also about to be brought home to Peter Beardsley. A footballer's career is short and nobody remembers the losers.

In an interview at this time Chris said honestly that there was no way he wanted to play in the Second Division again. He had his taste of the sort of opposition, flair and support that Liverpool, Everton and Man United brought with them. The headline in *The Mirror* was 'If they're down, I'm off.'

Jack Charlton's continual plunges into the transfer market did not help. For a while he tried to buy the giant, George Reilly but failed so he went out and bought Tony Cunningham from Sheffield Wednesday. The rumour was that Charlton had never seen him play and indeed walked right past him at the station because he had no idea that he was black. Then out of the blue Reilly became available and so enamoured was Charlton with him that he bought the tall striker as well as Cunningham, thus ending up with two centre-forwards both over six foot. Neither was particularly renowned for speed or ball control. The day after Reilly was signed the manager had to ask him his name to write it on the blackboard.

Charlton decided that as he had bought the two big strikers he was committed to play them both with Waddle on the left and Beardsley on the right.

Chris asked why but never received an answer. The general idea was to get Chris and Peter round the back banging in the crosses with the two strikers scoring. Eventually it was all long stuff with Peter and Chris not getting a kick as it was too obvious. In fact at the end of the season the Newcastle scoring list read Beardsley 17, Waddle 16, Reilly 3 and Cunningham 1. Chris had scored 15 of the 16 goals before either Reilly or Cunningham had come. The statistics spoke for themselves though Charlton appeared not to listen. Chris feels one of the strikers should have been played, with himself and Peter playing off him.

The side staggered through February. In a match against Watford they were 2-1 up with the manager screaming at them to keep the ball and waste time. Beardsley could not play like that. He went on a run, whipped the ball in and Megson scored. United won 3-1 but after the game Jack still went mad particularly singling out Peter for his attack.

It was time to get away. Chris was tired of the Charlton system and tired of the Press. It had started in September when one paper had said his contract was up and then mushroomed. Every time it was 'Good goal' – 'Good game' – 'What about your future?' Wherever he went, even shopping, somebody would ask 'what are you doing?' To the shy intensely private player it was all too much. For the first time in his life he wanted to break out from the insularity of the North-East. By March 1985, it was really just a question of where he would go.

# CHAPTER 25

Before the transfer market officially became interested in Chris, his price was to increase because every club is prepared to pay more to have an England International in its ranks. It puzzles Chris to this day how a price for a player is arrived at. Is it the club or the Press? Young men such as Paul Gascoine and Tony Cottee get a £2 million price tag hung round their necks like an albatross when all they want to do is play football.

In January Chris had been invited to a full England Squad get together, but to his disappointment that had to be abandoned because of bad weather. His consolation was to spend a few days in Benidorm on a package deal with Jack Charlton and the rest of the squad.

In February he was rung up by the Press and told he had been called up into the England Squad named to play Northern Ireland. There had been so much talk beforehand that the news itself was almost an anti-climax. Yet when he heard it confirmed on the radio he felt an enormous pride, not just for himself but for all his family. He is never one for getting over excited, always trying to take life as it comes. If he ever scored the winning goal in the World Cup he would be over the moon when it happened but would never dream of running around afterwards shouting his mouth off. Not for Chris Waddle 'the hand of God' – rather the appreciation of the talent God gave him in his feet, particularly his left one!

On February 23rd, the weekend before the international, Newcastle played Luton and won 1-0 to consolidate their mid-table position. Chris drove down with Mick Harford – who would have to wait three years for his international call up, and joined up with the Squad on Sunday. Most of the players knew what it was like to be the new boy and generally everybody was very friendly.

Chris knew Alan Kennedy from the North-East and took some comfort in hearing another Geordie accent.

# WADDLE

The Squad flew to Belfast on Tuesday. Obviously there was some concern about playing in Northern Ireland but there was a lot of security and since that first trip, Chris has visited more volatile places at more dangerous times.

This was also the occasion Chris was to meet for the first time somebody whose name was to be linked with his in a way he could not then have conceivably imagined – Glenn Hoddle. There had already been some rumours linking his name with Spurs and all Glenn said was that if Chris ever decided to come South he should give him a ring and that Tottenham was a great club.

By February 1985, Bobby Robson had a settled side and a settled training routine. There was a warm up with Don Howe, then shooting practise, whilst the day before the game it was mainly set pieces. Chris was handed the number 16 shirt and kept it even though he did no more than warm up from the substitutes bench. The match was played at 100 miles per hour, England won 1-0 with a goal from Mark Hateley and the game ended with bottles flying in all directions.

Transfer rumours abounded. At the start of the season Chris had appointed Alastair Garvie, the former assistant secretary of Newcastle United as his agent. The two of them were very much alike, quiet, honest and reliable. Alastair is a tall Scot with a background in accountancy and an eye for young talent.

He was so impressed by Chris that he felt it worthwhile giving up a secure job with the First Division Club to further the career of the young player he had watched in awe since the first day he pulled on a black and white shirt. Now he is the agent for another such young player, Paul Gascoigne. They say lightening does not strike twice but certainly not many people could lay claim to spotting the embryo talents of two such players as Waddle and Gascoigne.

Chris was building his own team around him. He had appointed the writer as his lawyer and Lennard Lazarus, a partner in the West End practice of Arram Berlyn Gardner & Co, as his accountant. When the time came he would be ready. This time there would be no question of him signing whatever was put before him. Alastair would tell Chris who was interested in him for there was a lot of paper talk. He had been linked with most Clubs in the First Division and Real Madrid abroad.

If his relationship with his professional advisers was blossoming, the relationship with Jack Charlton was not. At Hillsborough against Sheffield Wednesday, the home fans were continually taunting, the abuse aimed principally at Chris. He waved to the

110

fans and the manager promptly substituted him. He gave as the reason the fact that Chris was not playing as well as he could. Chris got on the team coach with a huge bottle of whisky. 'What are you doing with that?' Charlton asked with a touch of envy. 'I got the man of the match award,' the player replied. Charlton said nothing.

Chris kept his place in the England Squad for the home match with Eire, stayed overnight at George Reilly's flat in Hemel Hempstead and then drove to High Wycombe. John Barnes, who had a hold on the left-wing position, was out of the Squad through injury and on the Tuesday Bobby Robson told Chris that he was playing. England won 2-1 through goals from Trevor Steven and Gary Lineker and, despite the attentions of Chris Hughton, Waddle had a steady debut. Afterwards Bobby Robson made a point of telling him he was quite pleased and that there was every chance there would be a next time.

It is always difficult playing against another British team – as was so dramatically demonstrated recently in Germany. Although not politically British the Republic of Ireland team contains players from British club sides, which gives matches between Eire and England something of a League fixture flavour.

It was Chris' first time at Wembley and when he went to warm up 45 minutes before the game he realised just how huge a stadium it was. He came off the pitch and was interviewed by ITV for their *Mid-week Sports Special*. He was the man of the moment, he could no longer afford to be shy, he had to talk and he found out it was not quite as painful as he had thought.

Newcastle seemed transfixed by what was happening to the Waddle career. Jack Charlton's attitude was strange. He had done some good positive things for Chris' career – he had let him play as a striker, persevered with him and then reversed the situation. Perhaps his main problem was that he always treated the club's money as his own and therefore, understandably, did not wish to spend too freely!

He was also his own man and made it clear to the Board they could not override his decisions. He made an offer to Chris in respect of a new contract, but it was insulting.

Chelsea were the first of many to make an offer to Newcastle and eventually Chris tired of reading about his fate in the newspapers. He decided to take it into his own hands and went to see Stan Seymour with whom he had always enjoyed a really good relationship. It was on a Wednesday night after a reserve match.

# WADDLE

Stan sat in the manager's office exuding the fatherly feeling that Chris always seemed to bring out in him. 'I've decided I'm leaving.'

Stan was loath to let his talent go and promptly increased the manager's offer. Chris told him that although he appreciated it, it had come too late – the higher offer should have been made from the start. He did not like the idea that the Club had been trying to negotiate to keep him cheaply. 'Where do you want to go?' Stan asked. He told him Chelsea and Tottenham had made a bid. It was not a difficult decision. He remembered what Glenn had said about Spurs, he liked the idea of joining a Club that had actually done the double in his lifetime and he felt that they were a club striving to achieve things. The overriding factor, of course, was that he liked the way Spurs played the game. He told Seymour who said 'alright, you will be a Spurs player by the end of the week. We will call you out of training and you can go down to agree terms.'

On Thursday Chris trained normally and then waited for the car to take him to the plane that Spurs laid on to fly him to London. Nobody came. In desperation, he 'phoned the writer. It was decided that it would be made quite clear to Newcastle that Chris had no intention of re-signing for them and a note to that effect was given to Russell Cushing.

Stan Seymour called Chris to his office once again. He was now apologetic for reneging, but firm. 'I can't be the one who lets you go – you will have to stay to the end of the season.'

Looking back on it now, Chris doesn't know if he would have stayed had the Club dealt fairly with him as soon as the transfer rumours began. There were other players getting more. After Chris departed, Peter Beardsley was offered £2,000 per week to stay, a sum Chris feels he was well worth. He has never been one to make money his God but he knew what he was worth and it was a lot more than Newcastle were offering. The hard thing was being the first one to go. Everybody tried to come out of it looking the cleanest. The Club claimed they had offered the player what he wanted but omitted to say when they had made that offer. It was a husband calling to his wife long after the door had shut behind her, long after his marital infidelities. There is a time in every relationship when it is too late to kiss and make up, too late to turn back.

112

# CHAPTER 26

Chris had to accept that he could not go till the end of the season but events did nothing to soften the disappointment. Spurs were third in the League with a lot of home games to come; as it transpired if they had won them all they would have won the League and Chris would have liked to have been a part of that challenge. As it was, the transfer deadline passed and Chris remained a Newcastle player.

It was not easy staying in the North-East when everybody knew he was leaving. Injured for the Sunderland match, Chris went to see Whickham play in the FA Vase. In the bar afterwards chatting to the lads, a photographer came in from *The Journal* and asked for a picture. Chris refused and the man seemed to accept the position. Then when Chris wasn't looking he took the picture anyway. The papers carried the story of the goalless draw at Sunderland and pointed out where Chris had been. It was one of the rare occasions when he really lost his temper, evidence that by then the pressures were beginning to tell. Perhaps it was his own fault, as if he'd gone to the Sunderland match he'd have been beyond reproach.

Against Liverpool, Jack Charlton invented another system with everybody in a straight line and nobody forward. It was very frustrating and although Newcastle came back from 1-0 down to equalise, they still lost in the end. They beat Southampton 2-1 and Chris felt he was still giving of his best despite the headlines that read 'I'm off'. The fans were unappreciative and he was resoundingly booed. It hurt, but he could understand it.

As fate would have it, the last home game in the season was

against Spurs. He felt very uncomfortable and probably should not have played. If he gave a bad pass he could sense the crowd thinking – 'He's passing to them already' and he began to regret that perhaps he had said too much too early.

Spurs players, on the other hand, were much amused. Paul Miller was left for dead and when he finally caught up said 'come near me so that I can kick you before you sign for us.'

The game ended in a draw with Glenn Hoddle scoring from a great free kick and Chris not getting the goal he wanted to leave behind in the fans' memories. He walked off the pitch with his head down not knowing whether to wave or clap less it be misconstrued. He felt sad and confused, puzzled as to why he should be leaving on such bad terms.

He went into the players lounge and was joined by all the Spurs players. He felt like a visitor. Paul Miller never one to miss an opportunity said to Charlton 'hello Jack, nice to see you at a game – I thought you would be fishing.' Jack was not giving up. Knowing he had lost the player, he still tried to influence his decision before he signed. 'You should go to Chelsea – they have offered more money.' None of that made any difference to Chris, he pointed out that he didn't want to go to Chelsea but was happy to join Spurs.

He was leaving because he thought he had a better future there than Newcastle. Chris sat with Ray Clemence, Paul Miller and Graham Roberts. The rest of the team showed no hard feelings. He had crossed the line.

Within days he was to receive the Player of the Year award from Bobby Robson and the *News of the World* Player of the Year Trophy. He was second in the PFA Young Player of the Year and in the top five of the actual PFA Player of the Year. Chris explains the apparent anomoly by saying players didn't realise how old he was!

In the middle of his last week, he threw a leaving party for the players at a restaurant in the city centre. George Reilly, having crashed his car, wearing a collar around his neck and displaying a row of broken teeth won the fancy dress prize of the night with his impression of Dracula. Everybody came without exception. It was a good night.

The last match of the season was at Norwich. Chris went over to take a corner and John Dodds, a Newcastle-mad kid shouted 'Waddley, give us yer shirt'. He did and then went home.

On the 14th May, as a free agent with his contract at Newcastle at an end, Chris came down to London to White Hart Lane. Spurs and Newcastle had almost inevitably failed to agree terms and it was referred to the FA Tribunal that decides the fee in such cases. Spurs manager Peter Shreeve greeted Chris warmly. It had been a long wait. He showed Chris and Lorna around the mighty stadium and the new stand and facilities all seemed so much better than those he had been used to. If it was a far cry from St James' Park, it was a million miles from Tow Law, a million miles travelled in such a short space of time. While Chris was being shown around, Irving Scholar sat down with Chris' professional advisers to hammer out the terms. At the end of the day there were only a few outstanding details. The Club wanted the player, the player wanted the Club, everything went smoothly and amicably, the loose ends would be tied up when Chris got back from Mexico for he had already received a letter inviting him to join England's trip to Mexico and the USA.

Although he had not formally signed, he left for that tour a Spurs player in everything but name. It was only rubbing salt in the wound for the North-East Club, its officers and directors to see the word 'Newcastle' in brackets after his name for those international matches.

Before the tour there was a game in Finland. John Barnes still had first run on the left-wing berth and started the matches. In fact, on that occasion, Chris replaced Trevor Steven and played on the right. He didn't care where he played as long as he wore an England shirt. It was a relief to get away even though his view of Finland was limited to seeing the film *Witness* with Finnish sub-titles.

Lorna was not idling. The house in Newcastle was on the market and she came down to stay with the writer and his family in order to go house hunting chauffeured around by Harry, the Tottenham general helper. Eventually she got the choice down to two or three, finally settling on the house where they live now in Broxbourne. Chris was happy to leave that sort of thing to his wife. He was staying with the England Squad who were off to play Scotland.

They stayed at Troon where he was introduced for the first time to the pleasures of golf. He had still not been introduced to the pleasure of actually starting an international. Again he came on as a substitute, excited to take part in an England-Scotland encounter, and managed to set off on one jinky run. He should have shot.

## WADDLE

Arthur Cox would have been screaming at him to do so. Instead he went to the byline and put in a cross. Bobby Robson was encouraging saying that he looked lively when he came on. Everything was set for him to play a full ninety minutes.

# CHAPTER 27

He had never been to South America even in his dreams. He found himself rooming with Mark Hateley, a lively character whose total lack of fear earned him the nickname 'Psycho'. Chris got on well with him. Mark liked to joke and whatever had happened on the pitch, he would always be prepared to throw his arm around an opponent at the end of the game.

The hotel sold beer by the yard or half yard. Whenever Bobby Robson gave permission a group of the players, notably Kenny Sansom, Glenn, Chris and Mark would buy a couple of measures. In his article in a National newspaper, Mark called them the 'Yard Squad'.

He was becoming much friendlier with Glenn. The team tended to divide into packs of 5 or 6 and Glenn and Chris had similar interests, particularly music. They both led the same sort of life sticking with their old friends rather than mixing exclusively in football circles.

The first game of the tour against Italy saw Chris starting the match with Barnes on the substitutes bench. As was so often to be the case, the one who started disappointed and his replacement did better. Mark Hateley scored, although England lost 2-1.

It was very hard playing at altitude. Training had started with 12-minute runs and then one afternoon there was a cricket match, of all things against the Reform Club, an English expatriate enclave. Everybody played in white. Gary Lineker hit about 50 and Chris only fielded but thoroughly enjoyed the day, and the locals looked on and, not for the first time, thought the English were mad.

The Barnes-Waddle situation took on Tweedledum-Tweedledee like proportions when, against Mexico, Chris replaced John. England lost 1-0 and heads were down a bit, then they defeated Germany 3-1, a score which mirrored Chris' best England performance up to then. It is quite incredible that two years later nothing has changed in the alternative selection of the two wingers, and it is a tribute to both their natures that they remain the best of friends.

Bob Harris, in Mexico City writing for the *Evening Chronicle*, headlined his article of 13 June 1985: 'Waddle wins his spurs.' He went on to say, 'Newcastle United's Spurs-bound striker Chris Waddle finally came of age here in Mexico City yesterday. Waddle, playing only his second full game, was a key figure in England's biggest victory over their great West German rivals for 50 years. Manager Bobby Robson said, 'this was easily his best match for England.' He looked fitter and stronger than before and played with great tenacity and a lot of confidence, he grew in stature as the game progressed. He is a big boy, over 13 stone, and at first he looked as though he might not take to the conditions. But when he got going he looked very quick and clearly improved with acclimatisation.

The difference was that this time Waddle was not restricted to his left-wing role and switched freely from flank to flank ... [this] versatility ... will stand him in good stead in the future, even to the extent of promoting him above the unpredictable John Barnes.'

One of the problems then – and even now – is that Chris doesn't look like a footballer, or indeed any sort of sportsman. Although he appears slouched he has no real weight problem. Until he was 17 he was tall and thin, then suddenly he filled out and since then has clocked in at a steady 13 stone, and is 6' 1' when he stands up straight!

Chris' game blossomed in Mexico. Bobby Robson gave him the freedom to go from side to side and, oddly enough, on that tour he played better on the right-wing. He was much more mature, not just as player but also as a person, less an individualist and more of a team player. The trip was rounded off by a 5-0 victory in Los Angeles and it was back home to the excitement and preparation of a new season with a new club.

# CHAPTER 28

It was always going to be difficult breaking ties with the North-East. When Lorna first came down south she was met at Kings Cross by Marilyn Stein, the writer's wife. Travelling to Southgate on the underground a young man continually eyed up the two women. Finally he spoke: 'Aren't you Lorna Waddle?' He turned out to be nothing more harmful than a Newcastle supporter. It seemed there was no escape!

Chris came south on a permanent basis and stayed at the Pondesbourne Hotel in Hertfordshire while Lorna remained in Newcastle to sell their house. House prices in the south were a shock. Their own property had appreciated only a couple of thousand of pounds in two years, whilst further South they found they had to pay six figures for anything half-way decent. Tottenham, as ever, were helpful. As Chairman Irving Scholar always says, 'We refuse to let anybody joining the Club from outside London be classed as the poor relation.'

Scholar also accompanied Chris and Peter Shreeve, the then Spurs manager, to the Tribunal. In these days of freedom of contract, when a player's contract expires and his club cannot agree a fee with the purchasing club, the matter is referred to an independent Tribunal which fixes the price. The purchasing club is then obliged to pay that price, the old club to accept it. Newcastle United were represented by Stan Seymour (Chairman), Russell Cushing (Secretary), Jack Charlton (Manager), and Gordon McKeag (then simply another Director, himself a solicitor and now Chairman and Member of the Football League Committee).

The clubs put their cases, Newcastle's being argued for three-quarters of an hour. Then it was Chris' turn.

'Why do you want to leave Newcastle?'

'I want to better my career. I feel I have more of a chance of European and International honours with Tottenham.'

They then asked if he had anything particular to say, he did.

There was an old debt to pay, one he felt Newcastle had failed to honour; he told the Tribunal that he'd like Newcastle to pay Tow Law something if they got a good fee for him because Tow Law had no flood lights. There was an adjournment and then they were all summoned back in. Newcastle had been looking for £750,000 and Spurs felt that anything under £600,000 would be a bonus. The Tribunal decided on £590,000. Someone thought the length of the Newcastle submissions had cost them £10,000! The Tribunal also added that Chris had said he would like Newcastle to look after Tow Law. He does not know if they ever did, but in any event, the Newcastle contingent said a cold goodbye and got into the car without so much as wishing him good luck. It was an unsavoury ending and one that did much to assuage any lingering doubts Chris may have had about leaving his native North-East.

He began to train with Spurs after a painful tooth extraction. During the operation in Newcastle, the tooth had snapped and had to be drilled out; yet nothing was going to stop him getting super fit for the new season. He had a lot to prove to a lot of people. Paul Allen had also been signed on in the close season from West Ham. Once the youngest player ever to appear in a FA Cup Final, his career had slightly lost its way and he welcomed the opportunity to join his cousin Clive at White Hart Lane.

Peter Shreeve and John Pratt were generally in charge of the training but Mike Varney the physio was responsible for the warm-up. This took the shape of aerobics in front of two speakers. Chris was terrified as every day for a week Varney summoned four or five of the players up front. Chris would watch mad Lizzie on Breakfast Television to try and get ideas but perhaps Varney realised the player's intense shyness for he always allowed him to hide at the back.

Before he knew it, the pre-season friendlies had started. The first time he pulled on a Spurs shirt was against Wycombe Wanderers at Bisham Abbey.

He played up front with Clive Allen who promptly picked up an injury that ruled him out for a great chunk of the season. Chris, however scored in a 5-1 win and scored twice more against Chesterfield. The team moved out to the South coast, lost to Plymouth, drew with Exeter (not a favourable ground for Chris – and yet again he was substituted – this time without even seeing the pretty physiotherapist) and beat Bournemouth 3-1. It was then back to London for Glenn Hoddle's Testimonial and his first taste of a North London Derby against Arsenal. It was different from the games against Sunderland but nonetheless impressive for even in an atmosphere where nothing was at stake, you could feel the fans not wanting to give an inch. Fortunately for all concerned, the final result was 1-1.

The season proper started with a game against Watford. Chris played up front this time along side Mark Falco. Spurs won 4-0 and Chris got two of them, both headers. It was a really good atmosphere in the dressing room and for the first time in his career, he felt that perhaps he was actually going to be part of a team destined to win something.

Danny Thomas met up with him and was obviously pleased to welcome him but there was the problem of what nickname to give him. Professional footballers are obsessed with nicknames – often doing the journalist's job for them. Chris kept a low profile until Glenn Hoddle opened his mouth and said he had been known as 'Widdley'. Chris groaned but they all started calling him Widdley and there was nothing he could do. The rest of the players teased him gently about his accent and, claiming they could not understand what he was saying, asked him to slow down, demanded Mickey Hazzard from Sunderland to act as an interpreter. Despite their friendliness, Chris found the first year difficult. He was still shy, still scared to interrupt a conversation, still only prepared to respond when he was spoken to.

After the thrashing of Watford the season became a bit patchy. They drew away to Oxford 1-1 with Chris having two chances, one of which ex-Newcastle's 'keeper, Steve Hardwick, kicked away with his foot just for old time sake. A defeat at Ipswich and an injury to Tony Galvin found Chris stuck on the left-wing and although he scored twice against Sheffield Wednesday, he knew that he could play better than he was.

Before the Newcastle game a story broke that he could well have done without. He was talking to Jack Steggles of *The Mirror* who asked if there were any real differences between the Clubs. Chris said no, they were both big Clubs but that Spurs were not only fulfillling their potential but also looked after their players better. At Tottenham there were fresh kits every day whilst Newcastle made even the first team make do with the same kit the whole week; at Newcastle the players got fresh fish and chips on the coach whilst Spurs provided a three course meal geared to the individual's requirements. The story was given a huge headline in Newcastle and as Chris came onto the pitch, he was greeted with cries of 'Fish and Chips', 'Judas'.

# WADDLE

Alan Davies scored a great goal to put Newcastle in front and Chris thought it might be one of those days. Then Spurs hit back and ran out easy winners by 5-1. Kenny Wharton asked for a few cans of lager for the Newcastle players to drink on the coach. Chris duly obliged for his old team-mates.

The worst seemed over. He had played against Newcastle, his new team had won and he had shed no tears. He had crossed the great divide and, at least as far as he was concerned, he was now one of them.

# CHAPTER 29

Lorna and Chris settled in very well in their new surroundings. Lorna visited home fairly regularly and their old friends kept in touch by phone, not ringing every week but sufficiently to ensure that they kept up with the North-East scandal. For the Waddles it was a pleasure to go for a drink in the local at Broxbourne and not be bothered by autograph hunters, and troublemakers. Their lives were fast becoming their own.

He was chosen to play for England against Turkey. He got the ball on the left-wing and was going to give it to Gary Steven. However he kept knocking it past defender after defender, got to an acute angle and hit it into the net. Despite the efforts of some journalists to write him off from the World Cup because of alleged inconsistency, he felt a secure member of the England team, a team that had now qualified for the World Cup Finals.

They then played Northern Ireland, a match the Irish had to avoid losing to qualify for Mexico. Ireland played eleven men behind the ball and survived in a goalless draw mainly due to the brilliance of Pat Jennings. Rumours abounded about the match being fixed as England had nothing to lose. It was a nonsense of course as it is very hard to fix a match although Chris has had his suspicions when two communist teams draw. In all his career to-date, Chris has never been offered money to throw a game nor has he ever heard of anybody being offered a bribe. Even if one player has a bad game, there are still the other ten. Football is a well paid occupation unlike the situation during the great bribery scandal of the 60's when certain players were jailed and banned for life. It's simply not worth the risk.

In the run-up to Christmas Spurs' form did not really improve. They could not get a consistent run together and, while the fans had taken to Chris at first because he had scored in his debut match, the honeymoon was over. It was also his first Christmas in London. He and Lorna try and keep up with as many people as possible from the North-East and could hardly be accused of being ashamed of their roots or trying to forget them, and that Christmas they were certainly inundated with cards from old friends. But it was very quiet, just the two of them, and in a way he missed the travelling around with Newcastle. They spent most of Christmas Day at home and then, feeling lonely and homesick, he joined the Squad at 9.00 pm for an overnight stay in a hotel, prior to an 11.00 am kick-off.

Chris feels that there is a strong argument for a total football shutdown over the Christmas period for, say, two weeks. That would give players the opportunity to spend the holiday and New Year with their families and friends just like everybody else.

After losing 2-0 to Chelsea, where Dixon and Speedie impressed Chris with their brilliance, he had to turn his attention to his first really competitive Arsenal-Spurs fixture on New Year's Day. In fact he had never actually played in a Newcastle-Sunderland local derby, merely watched from the stand, compounding rumours at the time that he'd come out in sympathy with the Roker side. On New Year's Day 1986 neither North London team was doing particularly well and a goalless draw before 45,000 (5,000 less than capacity) was no great surprise. The abiding memory was Graham Roberts putting Charlie Nicholas in the Paddock. It was very slippery in the middle and Charlie stopped by the Arsenal dug out. He pushed the ball away but Graham kept running and collided with him, pushing him over the boards into the crowd. The Spurs supporters greeted the sight with glee: 'Who put Charlie in the stands? Robbo did, Robbo did,' they chanted.

The Littlewoods Cup (the renamed Milk Cup) was well under way at this stage. Portsmouth brought some 12,000 supporters with them and the Pompey chimes, one of the most impressive vocal refrains from football's litany, echoed around the ground. It took Spurs three matches to try to see them off and there was no doubt that the south coast side had the better of the contest, finally knocking the First Division side out at Fratton Park.

They went to Oxford where the pitch was a joke; ice with water on top where it had started to melt. Oxford took the lead and Spurs brought on John Chiedoze who, through a mixture of injury and ill fortune, never made the impact in the First Division that his talents deserved. Chris switched to the right-wing and raced past his old team-mate John Trewick. He crossed the ball, thought it had vanished into the crowd and then heard a cheer as Chiedoze somehow made contact and scored.

While all the papers at the end of the 1987/88 season carried banner headlines about the intentions of the likes of Waddle, Gascoigne, Hateley and Hughes, poor John rated only a single line stating he had been given a free transfer. Such are the vagaries of football, such the cruelty of the sport.

The replay with Oxford was also notable insofar as Chris scored the greatest goal that never was. He dodged between three Oxford players seeming to beat some of them twice, then jinked around the box and hit the ball into the net. He could not believe, cannot believe to this day, that it could have been given off-side. Although Glenn Hoddle was undoubtedly in an off-side position, there was no way he was interfering with play. On that day Chris was inspired and scored the first goal, with Clive Allen getting the winner.

Despite the Cup run the papers were starting to build a campaign against Peter Shreeve, and once the newspapers target a manager he is a marked man. Rumours abounded; Shreeve would go; Newcastle would re-sign Waddle. This latter keeps resurfacing every six months. In a recent visit to Newcastle the writer was amazed by the number of people who had absolutely first-hand knowledge of Chris' impending return to St James' Park. It was almost a shame to tell them that neither Spurs nor Chris knew anything about it.

Shreeve himself seemed to be an unlucky manager, with injuries forcing him into using many players. He had also come up through the ranks at the club and that created something of a status problem. Yet he was a good tactician and Spurs' Cup progress continued with a 5-0 defeat of Notts County, after a 1-1 draw. The County team contained Tristram Benjamin. Tristram had on one memorable occasion played against Newcastle with an upset stomach. A crunching tackle left him on the ground and the Newcastle player involved tried to help him up, assuring him that the injury could not possibly be serious. Tristram explained that he'd had a slight accident in his shorts and as he limped off a broad Geordie accent could be heard saying loudly, 'Ee the lad's melting.' However it all came to an end against Everton. They had lost there 1-0 at the start of the season and in the Fifth Round they were dismissed 2-1 at home.

Meanwhile there were all sorts of threats to Chris' England place. He and Glenn missed the fixture in Egypt and Peter Beardsley made his international debut, together with Gordon Cowans and Danny Wallace, all of whom did well. The competition was clearly no longer limited to John Barnes.

# WADDLE

Being away from Newcastle was no guarantee that the Press would not fabricate stories. Spurs organised a trip to Jersey which was wildly inaccurately reported as an orgy, with naked players cavorting along hotel corridors. In fact it was just a few days break. There was inevitably some drinking in the bar, but the worst of it was a player putting a lampshade on his head! But the Press would not let them alone and the alleged incident certainly attracted a considerable amount of publicity for the hotel. Chris, however, had to face a doubting Lorna who threw a newspaper article at him with the piercing question, 'what's all this then?'

Chris has never quite come to terms with the vivid imagination of some journalists. On one occasion he was reported to have been at Valentines with Richard Gough and Ossie Ardiles, yet he still doesn't know where the place is – or was.

Failure on the field seems to breed newspaper speculation. By March Spurs were out of both cups and eleventh in the League, compared to their runners-up position the previous season. It did not need a footballing expert to see the writing on the wall for Peter Shreeve.

Despite the pressures on Shreeve everybody enjoyed working with him. This is not always the case with managers who are going through a bad patch as far as the Press is concerned.

There are some who seem to want to speak out against every player just for the sake of attracting publicity. The good manager lets his team's results speak for him. Terry Venables often talks to the Press, but would never criticise any individual player. Arthur Cox is another who does a quiet solid job without the need for sensationalising in the newspapers.

March also brought the away fixture against Newcastle. In a season that had disappointed, Chris was really looking forward to it. The team went up on the coach and stayed at the Gosforth Park Hotel, the same hotel where, in a different lifetime, Chris had celebrated promotion with Newcastle and bid farewell to Keegan. There were the expected photographers when he arrived, but he tried to keep a low profile and just went out for a walk with his old friend Steven Preston. They got to the ground early and Chris saw a lot of guards around the players' entrance. Much amused, the rest of the Spurs team urged Chris off the coach first. Very reluctantly he descended to taunts of 'Judas' and as quickly as he could he sorted out his tickets and went to get changed.

It was really strange to be in the Visitors' dressing room and at first Chris thought he was in the wrong place. He was told to lead

126

the team out and, as he did so, the rest of them held back. It was only when he had run 20 yards he realised he was completely alone and once again the target of chants of 'Fish and Chips'.

Glenn scored a great goal which hit the stanchion and came out to allow Chris to ram it back in. The tannoy credited Chris with the goal and part in disgust, but more to do with a clash of heads with David McCreery, Glenn came off.

Newcastle drew level then Roberts whipped the ball in and Chris ran between Jeff Clarke and Glen Roeder. The keeper dived, the ball rolled along the line and ended up in the net. Chris actually ran towards the Gallowgate End which greeted him in total silence. There was no real animosity from the players although Glen Roeder had jokingly told him to 'cut it out' when he ran past him.

Having scored in two consecutive matches and feeling the season was at last having something to offer him, Chris went to join the England Squad at Luton on Saturday night for the long flight to Tblisi in Russia. He had his own preconceived ideas about life behind the Iron Curtain; everybody wore grey and walked about without a smile. He was not that far out. Upon arrival the squad had to stay in the waiting room for more than an hour and then had all their newspapers taken away from them. In what was supposed to be the best hotel, Chris found himself sharing a tiny room with Mark Wright. The towels were small and thin and it was almost impossible to dry himself after a bath in tepid water, the blankets had holes and worst of all there was only one television channel – in Russian of course!

England had taken some food with them such as baked beans, the players' favourite, but they tried the local soup which was like warm water with a potato dumped in it.

There was so little to do that in desperation Chris and some of the other players went to see a circus.

The game itself, a friendly, was played before a 90,000 crowd and much to their surprise, the English players got a standing ovation when they came out. It was later explained to them the locals regarded themselves as Georgian rather than Russian and hardly even spoke Russian.

Chris played a one-two to Peter Beardsley in his own half. Peter then dragged the ball back. Chris ran into the box while Gary Lineker went to the near post. Beardsley flicked it back and Chris hit it home. Although he was substituted by Trevor Steven after an ankle injury, the papers next day carried the headline 'Tiger of Tblisi'. How could anybody have known that two years later with

Chris not even on the substitutes bench, England would be annihilated by the same Russians as they bowed tamely out of the European Championships.

Russia was as much a mystery when he left as when he arrived. They were given no chance to speak to the Russians, neither to the public nor the players. There was nothing to buy there and all Chris brought back with him was a debilitating bug. Of all the places he visited in the world, the Soviet Union is one to which he does not want to return.

On his arrival back he had a photo session with Kenny Sansom at the airport because Spurs were due to play Arsenal on the Saturday. Then on the Friday a throbbing pain developed in his stomach and he could not retain food. He struggled through the match against Arsenal and got a bang on the head from David O'Leary for his trouble. After the game he was totally devoid of colour and energy.

He went into the players lounge and said to Lorna that he had to get home he felt so dehydrated. As quickly as it had come, the bug seemed to go away and in the absence of Glenn he played in central midfield against West Ham and Leicester.

He felt very tired after the Luton game and was then obliged to travel to Coventry to do the Budget Car Awards. He duly carried out his functions but the next day felt even worse than when he had returned from Russia. He could not even drive. Pat Nelson drove him back from the Midlands and Chris lay in the back of the car. All he could do when he got home was to sleep and have a mouthful of water and rush off to the toilet.

The Coventry visit was also the start of Chris' singing career but that must wait its turn in the story. Right now, Chris was still weak but felt well enough to play against QPR. After the match he not only felt tired but more depressed than at any time since his arrival in London. There was a charity function in the Chanticleer at White Hart Lane and Chris confided in Glenn that something just didn't seem to be right. Glenn told him to keep plugging away, that he had the skill, that it would happen. Confidence is an essential part of every footballer's make-up; if he hasn't got it he can't be effective. Chris doesn't think his confidence will ever be shattered again and even during the dreadful injury run of the 1987/88 season he always believed that he would not only be back in the Spurs team, but also on the plane to Germany for the European Championships.

In fact, Spurs and Chris picked up at the end of the season and scored 13 times with four consecutive wins to finish the year. Chris felt that a run of victories would be enough to guarantee the manager's position for the following season, that the basis was there, but that was with hindsight. Four youngsters had come into the squad but none made it. Cooke went to Bournemouth, Dick to Ajax, Bowen to Norwich and Leeworthy to Oxford. Only Howell of that season's debutants remains. Falco and Galvin also went and indeed of that Spurs team of just two years ago only Chris, Paul Allen, Hughton and Mabbutt survived.

This is another indication of the artificiality of the lives professional footballers lead. A career nowadays can take a player anywhere – and not just within the United Kingdom. He has to be ready to pack up his tents to go where the money is for the mine soon runs out once he has passed 30. There is no time, no room for close friendships during playing days, the Hoddle-Waddle relationship is the exception rather than the rule. A footballer of the 80's is a nomad, a mercenary, a carpet-bagger.

# CHAPTER 30

Chris had his confidence sufficiently restored to expect to get picked for Mexico. There was always the niggling doubt fuelled by the newspapers that somebody would be selected before him such as Peter Davenport, Danny Wallace or Gordon Cowans; but in April he duly received his invitation to the party and on the 6th May, he assembled with the rest of the squad, now almost one of the old guard.

There was a formal reception at Westminster with the Minister of Sport for which the squad wore their suits and ties, suits which they never wore again. Then there was the inevitable record and the even more inevitable appearance on Wogan where most of those singing seemed to be entirely unfamiliar with the words. Little was Chris to know that within a year he was to have his second entry in the top twenty.

It was off to Colorado. Although it was very hot and Chris is no great lover of the heat, he did like the place immensely. From there they went to play Mexico in a friendly and won 3-0 with Hateley scoring twice and Beardsley once. The wives joined them in Colorado for which they were all grateful and morale (and morals) were high.

Sharp as Bobby Robson was in his tactical approach to the game, he was very vague off the field. He would keep forgetting people's names and call Mark Hateley 'Tony' and say 'What's your first name again?' Dave Watson was a particular problem to him.

The England preparation however left no room for error. Nothing was left to chance, in 1970 there had been no medical tests but now regular blood and urine samples were taken. If the haemoglobins were high then the player would have to take iron tablets. After two days work in Colorado getting rid of jet lag, the players found themselves taking a 1½ hour walk up the mountain followed by a 15 minute run down. Chris had never run down the side of a mountain before (not many people have) and he found it positively exhilarating. Some of the players were not so heroic and walked down!

The papers were making more of his rivalry with John Barnes than the players. As far as they were concerned whoever was picked was picked and they could only do their best. The team played Canada and Korea and won 3-0 and 4-0 respectively. Chris didn't score and alternated with Barnes.

The week with the wives and girlfriends flew by, a week of golf and tennis, of watching movies and seeing Joanne Conway the British skater practice on the ice rink. It was the calm before the storm, the quiet in the trenches before the men had to go over the top at dawn. The FA took everybody out for a meal the wives and all, and then the women were packed off home. It was on to Monterey and the real thing was ever nearer.

The team was beginning to take shape. Shilton picked himself in goal but the right-back position was in dispute between Gary Stevens and Viv Anderson. In the back four Terry Butcher was a certainty but the remaining place was a choice of Fenwick (then QPR, now Spurs) and Alvin Martin of West Ham. Kenny Sansom was a certainty as was Lineker and Bryan Robson, if he kept fit. After that it was a question of take your pick – although Chris, at least, felt that Glenn Hoddle was a definite starter. Bryan Robson's shoulder had attracted more pre-tour publicity than anything else since its dislocation, yet in training he did not hold back. If it went, it went but he seemed to be very fit and as Bobby Robson's talisman he was vital to England's plans.

For the most part the team were in a separate hotel to the Press. Sunday was the official Press day. The same questions over and over again: 'How's the shoulder Bryan?' 'Is it you or Barnes?' – whoever it was good luck, Chris replied. He was just pleased to be there. Viv Anderson, for example, had been to two World Cups and never played while Kerry Dixon had had a bare 30 minutes against Poland. Poor Viv also went to Germany without getting a game and in years to come must be the subject of a quiz question as to which player has been selected for 3 major international tournaments yet has never kicked a ball in anger. To somebody who has never played any sport at the highest level, it is impossible to transmit the feeling, the importance, the pride of just being a part of it all.

The pressure was really on England for everybody fancied them to qualify from their group. It was easy for the tipsters to say, but nowadays there is no such thing as a straightforward international away from home. Poland could play, as could Portugal on their day, while Morocco were a totally unknown quantity. England's group were in Monterey and the team stayed up in the mountains at Camino Real 45 minutes from the city. Bobby Robson announced his team two or three days before the match and nobody moaned about being left out. It was one team, one squad, one country.

Glenn Hoddle and Kenny Sansom ran a book on the earlier matches and there were some sharp intakes of breath when the Russians won 6-0 and the.Danes looked devasting; but as Chris points out the World Cup is not about peaking early. Italy, in 1982 had a bad start and came through to win, and none of the England team were really encouraged by Germany's cautious opening in 1986.

The first fixture against Portugal was a near disaster. For a while it seemed as if their week of practice and rehearsal had been a total waste of time. There was no problem about possession but they just couldn't turn it into goals. Just after an hour Chris was substituted by Peter Beardsley. One English missed tackle meant a Portugal goal and a very unhappy manager. It was not the most auspicious beginning.

Bobby Robson tried to pick the team up. He hammered home the message – Morocco had drawn with Poland and if England won the two other games they were still through. Morocco had hardly impressed in the game against the Poles. Although they had a few players from the French League who worked hard for each other, they looked like a team who expected to achieve little in the competition.

There was a lot of press pressure on the manager to play Beardsley, dispense with wingers and drop Chris. He resisted but his luck was not about to turn. Bryan Robson's shoulder went, Wilkins was sent off and the message came to Chris to play as hard as he could down the right. Chris gave it all he had and finished the match totally exhausted and 5lbs lighter, surprised he had not been substituted. The game finished goalless and although England had done enough to win it, one solitary point from two matches – and that from a 0-0 draw with Morocco was hardly tournament-winning stuff.

The backroom staff came more and more into the picture. They were feeling the strain too. Dr Vernon Edwards, the team Doctor had already suffered a heart attack in Colorado although he came on to Mexico later. Their part in the build up to England's matches

132

is always much underrated. Fred Street, the team physiotherapist had six years of practical experience at a London hospital and then moved into professional football with Stoke City. In 1971 he was invited to join mighty Arsenal and three years later he became the England physio and has now assisted at well over a 100 internationals. He himself had an assistant in the shape of Norman Medhurst whose father, Harry had suggested he join Chelsea as his assistant trainer in 1966. Twenty years later he was still there, by then the longest serving member on the staff at Stamford Bridge. he succeeded his father in 1974 and was invited onto the international scene in the same year.

The backroom team gave the squad the continuity that was inevitably lost as players came and went. Fred was heavily involved strapping everybody up, the Doctor doing blood tests, taking urine samples, even acting as a surrogate father by checking the players in their rooms at night. He always had a smile on his face, always friendly and approachable. Norman Medhurst was never above sorting out boots and kit or even clearing up after the players. Nothing had been left to chance. Mike Kelly was there as a specialist goalkeeping coach. Curiously enough in view of what happened at Wembley in 1988, he had begun as a 'keeper with Wimbledon and had also won a Cup medal with them, albeit an amateur one, in 1963. He was not without professional experience through having been with QPR and Birmingham. His official title was as goalkeeping coach to the England team and the FA/GM National School. In Mexico he spent much time with Gary Bailey, who sadly had to give up the battle against his injured knee shortly after and was forced into retirement. Street, Medhurst and Kelly – not names to conjure with like Waddle, Lineker and Beardsley, but just as vital to the team, appreciated by all the players even if virtually unknown to the public. Football is not just about footballers.

# CHAPTER 31

Meanwhile on the field the dice were beginning to tumble right for England. Poland beat Portugal and so did Morocco. England's destiny was back in their own hands and a win against Poland would see them through. The team selection for Bobby Robson posed hard questions. He was definitely without Robson and Wilkins and eventually decided on a 4-4-2 formation. He took Chris aside and told him he had done well, that he was not being dropped but he had to have a solid foundation. Chris was a player of flair and skill on the day but the manager obviously felt he lacked the necessary steel for such an encounter. It is another example of how even those extremely close to Chris can still fail to know and understand him. When the chips are down, he is as good a tackler as anybody, capable of following a manager's instructions to the letter.

He is now more philosophical, but in 1986 the fact that the manager told him not to worry about losing his place did nothing to stop the hurt; but at the end of the day Bobby Robson was the Manager and he had to make the decisions. Whatever Chris may have felt, the decision was more than justified on the field. England were 3-0 up at half time, Lineker had a hat-trick and the fans were doing congas around the stadium.

Chris etched his own little cameo into the World Cup by being sent on twenty minutes from time to replace Peter Beardsley accompanied by a handful of water bags. All that was missing were the goldfish! He went to go on the pitch with a few in one hand when Bobby Robson said take a few more. The few in this case meant about twenty. He put them down on the halfway line and chased the Polish centre-half and then returned to retrieve them, and tossed them to the English players. As each lad caught them, to a bag, they broke. When he got back to Spurs he was given a bag full of water and told: 'You left this in Mexico and they sent it over.'

Safely ensconced in the second round, despite the lack of whole

134

water bags, the team flew from the beauty of Monterey to the pandemonium that was Mexico City to meet Paraguay. The flight was a nightmare as the plane was buffeted so badly by thunderstorms that they had to stop and refuel. Everybody laughed about it afterwards but there were few smiles on their faces at the time and Chris Woods, who hates flying at the best of times, was nearly frightened to death.

The hotel in Mexico City was not much better than the plane. It was on a main road and whereas the team had been used to satellite TV this one only had a couple of local channels. It took all of ten minutes for Chris' withdrawal symptoms to set in as far as the television was concerned – not that they could have heard the television at night anyway. The traffic noise was incredible. They lasted just two nights there, two nights of broken sleep and then they moved out to the Holiday Inn where the Italian team was also staying.

This hotel was much nearer the level of luxury to which they had grown accustomed. It is strange how quickly players with modest backgrounds like Chris Waddle not only come to appreciate the finer things in life, but simply will not accept second best. It is not a question of false snobishness, but more a matter of experience. Who can blame them for demanding the best, when they know it is available and will be forthcoming? The Holiday Inn sported an indoor tennis court. John Barnes, Chris and Kerry Dixon decided to have a game. Barnes was on match point, Kerry went to whip the ball back and promptly cut his own eye with his racquet. The Press immediately pounced on the player and manager, demanding to know how it had happened and refusing to believe the absurdity of the true explanation.

The Italians in the hotel presented no problems. Mark Hateley knew some of them and was able to chat with them in their own language quite fluently. Vialli, their current superstar, had had his hair shorn for National Service. Chris thought Paolo Rossi the nicest of people and enjoyed listening to him and Mark talking. He was also very impressed by the Italian clothes, for the kit was stylish Diadora. If nothing else about the Continent appeals to Chris, the style and cut of their clothes certainly does. He contrived to swop shirts with one of the Italians, even though they didn't play them.

The Bulgarians were the complete opposite of the Italians, dull in their style and reminding Chris of his visit to Russia in their dress. It was no great loss to the tournament when they went out 2-0 to Mexico. If that match was a snore the Russia-Belgium thriller was enough to give anybody a heart attack. One-nil to Russia at half-time, 2-2 after 90 minutes, it finally went to Belgium 4-3 with Nico Claesen, who was to join Spurs, getting the winner.

Poland were demolished 4-0 by Brazil and then for once Argentina were the nice guys in beating Uruguay 1-0, a Uruguay team for whom the ball was a merely incidental when it came to kicking.

France showed much flair in beating Italy 2-0 with the infectious cry of 'Allez les bleus', but Germany were still struggling and only scraped home 1-0 to Morocco with a very late goal.

Then on the 18th June, England took on Paraguay in the Azteca Stadium and Chris wasn't even substitute. Bobby Robson told him he'd change the substitute for the next match but with sudden death there was no guarantee there would be a next match. Chris, sitting in a box in the stands alongside Kerry Dixon and the suspended Butch Wilkins, was left to ponder his international future. Wilkins' sending off had been regarded as a sick joke by his team mates. He had thrown down the ball and had accidentally hit the referee. As it happened, again, those who did not attend the party were not missed. It was 3-0 to England and three hundred World Cup minutes had past without Shilton conceeding a goal.

Without waiting to get on, Chris was able to analyse that particular match much more than most. Steve Hodge played well on the left and Glenn Hoddle was really inspired, as was Peter Reid. Beardsley was still playing on a high from the Poland game and the long-running partnership with Lineker was beginning to flourish. It surely must be a long time since England's front 2 were the first names to be pencilled in over a two-year period.

Even though they had played together at Newcastle, Chris and Peter were never very close. They were totally different people from different backgrounds yet in the build-up to the 1988 European Championships they began to room together and to understand each other.

Spain finished off the round by beating Denmark 5-1 and silencing even those English supporters who had latched onto the chant 'We are red, we are white, we are the Danish dynamite'.

It was down to the last eight and the feeling still existed that whoever beat Argentina would win the tournament. It was England who were drawn against them next. The trophy and the medals beckoned ever nearer and just at that moment in the third week of June 1986, there was no England player, least of all Chris, who did not believe that they could bring the World Cup home.

# CHAPTER 32

There were four days between the defeat of Paraguay and the match against Argentina and for Chris and the rest of the team there might just as well have been four years. They stayed on in Mexico City and were warned not to go out on the streets. Eventually in desperation and as an alternative to climbing up walls, they went out shopping en masse to a mall. They were told to be back by 6.0 pm but were caught up in the biggest traffic jam Chris has ever seen, and in fact did not get back until well after 8.0 pm, which did not please the manager.

One diversion was horse racing videos where they could show films of races without anybody knowing the results. Kerry Dixon and Peter Shilton were the bookmakers and as everybody knows, the bookies never lose. There was some training but in a way it was incidental. They went to a huge stadium where the pitch was much better than the one they had encountered in Monterey. They did some shooting, played some five-a-side, but there was a great confidence in the camp and if they hadn't got it right by now, they never would. The hotel pool saw as much action as the training ground.

The night before the match everybody was keyed up. Again Chris was disappointed to learn he was only to be substitute but he knew that from the tournament so far, he had every chance of getting on. At half-time it was goalless and very tight. It was all about mutual respect. England had a free kick and had heard that the Argentinians had a habit of running out when the kick was taken. Sansom dummied it. Hoddle took it and Sansom was there, only to be caught by an offside flag.

The Maradona 'goal' has been fully documented elsewhere but Chris himself thought at the time he had headed it when it went in and indeed only Barnes of the England players claimed handball immediately. There were enormous protests and Chris is adamant that a competent linesman should have seen it. Yet the way

137

Maradona ran away with his arms spread wide was very convincing. He kept running and didn't look back. However great a player he may be, on this occasion it seems he was nothing but a cheat. The second goal to Argentina, however, was unarguable and Bobby Robson told Chris to warm up and then to get on and put some crosses in. Peter Reid came off and suddenly England were playing again with two wingers. Barnes got to the byline twice. Once he got the ball across and Lineker scored and the second time the ball was kept out by a miracle. The second time the hand of God had protected Argentina that day.

In the dressing room everybody was livid. Although they had done as well as they could have expected in getting to the last eight, in retrospect Chris believes that they were capable of winning it. He returned a more mature player. He may have had a poor season going into the World Cup, and in that respect he realised he was fortunate to be there, but he also knew he had the ability and has always had sufficient faith in himself to believe it will come good on the day. He has the taste for the world scene and is determined to be back in Italy in 1990. He will only be 29, an age at which most midfield players are at their peak.

As an international player there was no real holiday. Chris accepts that, it's part of the responsibility however unfair it may be on your family. It was a far cry from being at Newcastle finishing in May and calling it a day until July. There was no sight seeing or relaxing afternoons for the England team. Originally they could have stayed for the Final but saddened and disillusioned, they thought there was no point and came home the day after they felt they had been conned out of the competition.

On his arrival back in England, Chris and Lorna went back to the North-East for a fortnight, their first real visit since he had joined Spurs. Once again he was struck by the lack of privacy. In London he can go into a pub or a restaurant without being pestered – it's not that he minds signing autographs but it's just that there's a time and a place for everything. In Newcastle, it had never stopped with an autograph. They always wanted to talk about matches and goals and when Chris is out with his wife for a drink, he does not want to talk shop. He has perfected a method of turning it around nicely. If somebody disturbs him, he will ask what they do for a living. If they're a bricklayer he will continue: 'How many bricks did you lay today?' 'What sort?' 'Were they breeze blocks?' 'What's your hod carrier like – lazy is he?'

Eventually they say they don't want to talk about it and at that juncture Chris has made his point.

The fans do pay their money which pays a player's wages but they don't own him and he is entitled to his privacy like everybody else. In the South it is far less of a problem. Often he doesn't get recognised and if he does, people keep their distance.

Recently Chris went to see Barnet play Windsor with the writer and was not even asked to sign a single autograph.

It's not just privacy that's different, it's the whole way of life. In the North-East the weekend out revolves around the social clubs – or the pubs: 'I'm just going out for a drink tonight.' In London there are more restaurants and despite the apparent formality, Chris finds it far more relaxed down in the South.

In a way, both Lorna and Chris were glad to get back home and they found it odd that they silently acknowledged that home was Broxbourne and not Gateshead. There is something very special about July in a footballer's life. Whatever has happened in the previous season is wiped out, the slate is clean. Even if you've just missed relegation you start level on points with the past season's champions.

For Tottenham the close season was one of change. Peter Shreeve's game efforts at the tail end of the season were not enough and David Pleat's appointment as Manager was announced when he was in Monterey reporting on the World Cup. He met with Chris, Glenn and Gary Stevens. 'What do we call you?' they asked. 'I don't care,' was the reply.

On the first morning back they chorused: 'Morning David.' He was not amused. The holiday was over. He was the Boss of Tottenham Hotspur Football Club and the players had to recognise it.

As a first step he brought with him Mitchell Thomas, the Luton left-back not renowned for his shyness, and it did not take Pleat long to instil his own brand of confidence in the team.

There was the normal round of friendlies including a visit to Spain where they came third in a tournament that included PSV Eindhoven, for whom Ruud Gullit was playing as sweeper. Spurs lost 5-4 on penalties when Van Bruecklen saved Glenn Hoddle's effort in a rehearsal for the 1988 European Championships.

Pleat made no dramatic changes from Shreeve's methods but tended to work on specifics like round the corner balls and following the pass. He inevitably brought in his own men like Trevor Hartley as coach and John Sheridan as physiotherapist. Their predecessors had done nothing wrong but when a manager falls this often means that his backroom team fall with him. It's unfair but its the way of life in the football jungle.

Pleat instigated a system of code words for moves; 'Sid' meant takeover, 'Jack' was 'let it go', 'Fred' signified a back heel. The first couple of weeks of this system were unbelievable. Chris would run with the ball and somebody would shout 'Fred'. He would have to stop to think what the hell that was and more often than not as he hesitated he'd lose the ball. By the start of the season the team had actually remembered who was what but when they came up against Luton in October, they discovered Pleat's old team still used the system. The only problem was their Fred was a Sid, their Sid a Jack. Anybody sitting near enough to the field of play to hear what was going on would have seen 22 baffled players shouting out first names which bore no resemblance to anybody on their programme. A month later against Norwich there was more confusion and one of the Norwich players asked in disbelief 'you don't use those stupid names as well?'

The season itself started really well. A 3-0 win away to Villa with Clive Allen scoring the first hat trick in the season that was to bring him 49 goals. Newcastle visited White Hart Lane on the Bank Holiday Monday. They brought with them their usual black and white horde who were taunted by the sight of Tottenham supporters burning £5 notes and chanting 'We're in work'. The replies were unprintable although the baiting of Chris was more muted. Allen scored again but a late equaliser by Beardsley in torrential rain against the run of play meant the points were shared. However, a 1-0 win against Man City with Graham Roberts scoring took Spurs to the top of the League. Everybody started to say that this was Tottenham's year and nobody wanted it to be more so than Chris Waddle.

# CHAPTER 33

Two weeks later after defeats by Southampton away, Chelsea at home and a goalless draw with Arsenal, the dreams were in tatters. Spurs had sunk to twelfth and seemed to be on the rocks. Yet it was not as black as it seemed. Southampton were always difficult to beat on their ground, a draw at Highbury was not a bad result and they had seen Richard Gough carried off against Chelsea.

Chris was going through a barren patch as far as scoring was concerned although he did not think he was playing badly. Clive Allen was playing upfront initially alongside Falco and then with Nico Claesen when he joined from Belgium in October. Pleat complained that there was not enough support for Allen in the box and because there were four in midfield, Chris found it difficult to get into a scoring position.

However, the team's recovery was steady. They beat Leicester away (Clive scored twice) then Everton at home (Clive scored twice) – this latter result reducing the writer's youngest son to tears as he sat in the Directors' Box. For reasons best known to himself, he's spurned all London clubs, rejected a lifetime of mind washing in the North-East tradition and plumped for Evertonian fanaticism. Those around him think he may grow out of it. Bobby Robson was moved to pat the disconsolate little boy on the head.

Luton came to White Hart Lane hyped up to do well against their old manager and held Spurs to a 0-0 draw in a bruising game. A trip to Anfield was on the agenda, Anfield that had been a wasteland for Tottenham teams over the years. In front of 43,139 fans including the huge travelling Spurs following, Clive Allen scored in a brilliant performance that could have seen Tottenham win 5-2. In fact, with Nico also demonstrating the skills that were allowed to shine all too rarely during his time with Spurs, they won 1-0 and moved up to third in the League.

Again, however, it was one step forward and several steps back. Mark Falco and Tony Galvin were both injured and suddenly it all started to go wrong again. A home draw with Sheffield Wednesday and then defeats by QPR, Wimbledon and Norwich saw them back down to eleventh by early November. Chris found it more frustrating than most. He had come to Spurs seeking success and the pattern of results was looking more and more like that which he had experienced at Newcastle. There was a narrow win against Coventry and then away to Oxford, the system suddenly changed. Clive Allen was left alone up front and Chris found himself one of five in midfield with additional freedom. It was like Samson unchained. They beat Oxford 4-2, Chris scored twice and Clive got the other two.

As far as Chris is concerned, Clive Allen is the best player he has ever seen at the near post. Chris would whip the ball in and Clive would score with a little flick. Not many forwards can actually run to the near post and get the ball because it's usually the defenders who get to it in that position. Clive was an all round player, at his best an excellent finisher and his strange loss of form in the 1987/88 season was a mystery to Chris as well as to the rest of the team. It all suddenly dried up and it's to be hoped he discovers the way to goal in France. All in all, not many players can say they have changed clubs three times in their career for sums in the region of one million pounds per transaction.

After Oxford, although Spurs lost at home to Forest 2-3, Pleat was not unhappy. It had been a great game, full of good football and one that had sent the fans home entranced and the pundits satisfied. As far as he was concerned, that was enough. The Forest game was followed by a 3-3 thriller against Manchester United. On television yet again Spurs were 2-0 down at half-time yet came back in a marvellous advertisement for the game from both sides. David Pleat had been a winger himself and understood that some of Chris' runs and dribbles would end up down blind alleyways; but the ones that got through and ended in a telling cross were worth it. That, perhaps, is something Bobby Robson has not appreciated either with Chris or John Barnes.

There seems little point in playing attacking players such as these in semi-defensive roles. The left-back is there to defend not the left-winger. Chris feels his game is best played with long mazey runs, some of which work and some of which don't. He is least effective when playing back or sideways. He is never worried when he is dispossessed because he knows there'll be somebody behind to fill in the gap – Chris is always looking forward to the next run down the touchline, the cross and the dead ball line, the positive rather than the negative side of the game. When he is allowed to blossom and develop at what he does best, which David Pleat allowed him to do, he will show the international audience what he has done time and time again at club level.

Spurs at the end of 1986 were beginning to get things together and they beat Watford, Chelsea and West Ham decisively. They also went on a Club trip to Bermuda staying at the magnificent Hamilton Princess. It was more a holiday than an official tour and although they played the Bermudan national team on Wednesday night, they also played golf a few times.

It is not possible to hire a car in Bermuda. The narrow winding roads have led the authority to restrict cars to the locals – and then only one per family. Tourists have to use either taxis or the mopeds that cause an average 3 deaths a year. Nobody told Mitchell Thomas that fact and he was the only one of the Spurs party brave (or foolish) enough to hire a bike. On one occasion Chris and a couple of other players were in a taxi with Mitchell following them. They knew he had no idea where the hotel was and told the driver to make a right. They then asked him to do a U-turn while all the time watching a bemused Mitchell Thomas from the rear window desperately trying to manoeuvre his bike to keep up with them.

Mitchell also became a legend in his lifetime on the Bermudan golf courses although he didn't play. Chris was having a round with Glenn and inevitably ended up in the rough. Chris shouted across to Glenn who had played his shot expertly, to ask what club he should use and Glenn asked Mitchell to drive him over. Chris leant casually against a tree and then saw Mitchell flying down the hill in the buggy at an impossible speed for so small a vehicle. Chris yelled at him to stop then leapt out of the way. Glenn flew out in slow motion and Mitchell, buggy and all went straight into the tree trunk. There was a huge dent in the vehicle but worst of all, it was stuck and however hard they tried, none of them could turn the wheel. Eventually they got the buggy free and Mitchell drove it back up the fairway oblivious to the fact that a loose bit of metal was churning up the turf like a farmer's field. People yelled at him and he cheerfully waved back. The man in charge of the greens looked at his buggy almost in tears. 'What happened?' he asked. Mitchell thought quickly, 'I heard someone shout "fore," went to avoid the ball and drove straight into the tree.' The story seemed to satisfy the man who gave Mitchell another buggy. They went back to the course and this time Mitchell parked it on the top of the hill overlooking the sea. As Glenn played a shot they heard a click as the handbrake went and saw the buggy rolling towards the ocean. The three of them dashed after it and several million pounds worth of footballers, as if in a movie, caught it just in time. There was no way that Mitchell could have explained that one away!

During the trip Chris roomed with Graham Roberts. Although the two had become good friends, Graham made no mention of his impending departure and on his return Chris and the other players were most surprised to learn he had decided to join Rangers. It was another example of how difficult it is for players to make and keep lasting friendships – although Graham has telephoned Chris on a weekly basis to keep in touch.

They were all tired when they got back but still beat Chelsea 2-0 and thrashed West Ham 4-1. Clive Allen could do no wrong and although the following season was disappointing, Chris still reckons that 70% of the time Clive will be on target with a shot.

They lost 3-2 to Coventry in what nobody then could have envisaged would be a virtual rehearsal for the Cup Final. They were consistently outjumped both in the front and the back, and Coventry's system of two aerial target men in attack was always a danger. Nico Claesen scored, as well as Clive, but was still doomed to be always in and out of the team. The system with one up front suited the side and there was no way the manager could take out a player who would score 49 goals before the season ended.

Christmas was lonely again. Newcastle was a long way off and there were just the two of them to celebrate. It was left to the football to give Chris what consolation there was and on New Year's Day a 2-0 win against Charlton took Spurs into fifth place in the League. If the Championship challenge was really to get into its stride then they had to win the televised game against Arsenal the following Sunday. It was easy to slip into the local derby feud. Even though Chris and the other Spurs players see many of the Arsenal players off the pitch and talk and mix with them, they cannot help but feel some satisfaction when the men from Highbury get beaten. As it happened it was Spurs who lost 1-2 on the 4th January, 1987 and Chris was getting the feeling that the odd goal of three would always fall to Arsenal when the two teams met.

Over the next five matches however, Spurs scored 12 goals in the League and conceded none. Only Scunthorpe in the Cup scored against them twice in a 3-2 defeat in which Chris scored Spurs' third. Despite the score Spurs never felt they would lose and there was a general premonition that this was the start of a Cup

Good omens for the 1988/9 season? Chris salutes the fans after scoring against Arsenal, September 1988
                                                                    *Photo: Action Images*

Waddle (No 11) beats 'keeper Hughes (Northern Ireland) in England's European Cup qualifying match, October 1986
*Photo: Action Images*

Chris Waddle of England taking on Gary Flemming of Northern Ireland in the European Cup qualifier of April 1987

*Photo: Action Images*

England v. Scotland at Hampden Park, May 1987 — Waddle powers a shot past McLeish (far left)
*Photo: Action Images*

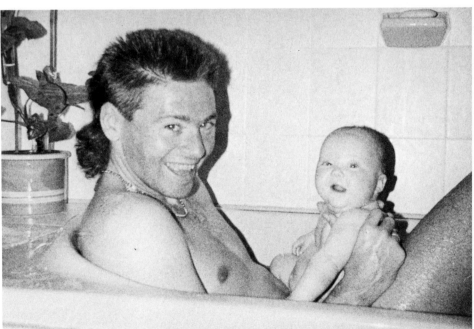

From the family album — Chris and his daughter Brooke

In relaxed mood with Glenn Hoddle at an England
training session

Rivalry? What rivalry? Pictured with John Barnes

Meeting Pele at the World Cup Finals of 1986 (Bryan Robson far left, Peter Beardsley to Chris' right)

In action for England against Brazil, May 1987

run. Chris has found that Tottenham are particularly wound up at the start of a Cup competition because of their tradition but that season it seemed to be even more the case.

In the fourth round Palace had a couple of early chances but then went down 4-0. Wembley always seems that much nearer to a team riding its luck. The fifth round draw brought more luck in yet another home tie but the opposition were somewhat more threatening, particularly as far as Chris was concerned – Newcastle United. Chris naturally was the centre of the pre-match build up and the pressure was on. United brought down with them the hordes of Geordie faithful, more than 10,000 in fact who still gave Chris stick but probably little more than anybody else. Spurs won 1-0 through a disputed penalty when Jackson was alleged to have pulled Mabbutt and although Newcastle were unlucky not to equalise at the death, it was the London club who were through to a sixth round tie against Wimbledon.

Meanwhile they had also been making steady progress in the Littlewoods Cup. They had beaten Barnsley, thrashed a weak Birmingham side 5-0 and won away at Cambridge. They drew at West Ham when they should have won and proved the point by beating them 5-0 in the replay.

That brought them face to face with Arsenal in the semi-final and on the 8th February they won 1-0 at Highbury in the first leg and with a home match to come they felt they had one foot at Wembley.

In the League they were on a roll as well and their 5-0 defeat of Leicester at the end of February saw them into fourth place. Chris was part of a free scoring team challenging for three sets of honours and in the early spring of 1987 his move to London seemed totally justified.

# CHAPTER 34

The 7th March 1987 was a fateful day for Danny Thomas, the same dynamic little player whose career had seemed so intertwined with that of Chris. The incident in the match against QPR is still the subject of legal action and cannot be described in depth here, but there is no doubt that Chris and the rest of the Spurs players were heart broken by the end result. Danny was carried off the field after a tackle by Gavin Maguire and rushed to hospital with his leg in a terrible state. Everybody in the Club went to see him and throughout it all he seemed very hopeful of getting back. Chris was enjoying playing with him and they had developed some good combinations. Danny was always prepared to do anything for anybody and was without doubt the most popular of players. When it was clear there would be no come-back it was hardly surprising that his testimonial raised so much money. Chris and everybody else at Tottenham are quite certain that he will succeed in his new chosen career as a physiotherapist.

It was not a good week for Tottenham because just six days before they had lost to Arsenal 2-1 after extra time in the second round of the Littlewoods Cup Semi-Final. That had taken the match to a replay on the Wednesday night when Spurs lost by the same score. It was Chris' most bitter disappointment in the game to-date. His mind had been full of thoughts of Wembley and then suddenly it had all slipped away from him. He just sat with his head in his hands and it did not really help to see Clive Allen crying as well; yet there was still the Wimbledon game to come the following week and Chris and the rest of the team had to pick themselves up.

It was about this time that things began to develop with the famous Waddle-Hoddle record. As mentioned earlier briefly, it all started at Coventry the season before. Glenn had not played but he and Chris found themselves up in the Midlands for an award ceremony and afterwards had a meal and a few drinks. Chris turned to Glenn and said 'we're up singing later.' Glenn replied

146

'no way' but their mutual friend Pat Nelson who was there arranged it and they did a passable version of *Hey Jude* that brought a request for an encore of *Can't buy me Love*. To his surprise Chris found he liked being in the limelight with everybody dancing and clapping in front of the stage and Pat told them it had sounded so good that he wondered if they would like to try and make a record. Chris and Glenn, without any real faith and encouraged by the wine, told him to go ahead and try to set it up. To their surprise, Pat took them seriously enough to set up a meeting with Bob Puzey, the well known song writer for the following Wednesday.

In the cold light of day, without the benefit of the wine, Chris was reluctant to go. Eventually, as he was doing nothing, he visited Pat and Bob and he and Glenn found themselves sitting on the settee singing *Daniel*. Bob Puzey then played a few songs he had written and asked them to listen to one in particular – *Diamond Lights*. It sounded totally different from the final record and they kept listening and finally began singing in Bob's bedroom while he fiddled with the mass of computers and keyboards that filled the room.

Before they began they both said: 'If it's rubbish don't be frightened to say so.' It wasn't rubbish – in fact it sounded almost professional and from then on it was just a question of getting a proper demonstration record made.

Chris, Glenn and Terry Hobart another friend, paid for the session at the Chocolate Factory in South London. They went in at 4.0 pm and went right through to 2.0 am. It was a lot harder work than it looked. The final mixes were finished the day after and when it was played to them, Chris and Glenn at least were impressed. That was when the real problem started. All this had taken place in August 1986, and Bob Puzey began the rounds of the record companies with his wife Kath. Because it was a finished record, the companies did not want to know, and even those who showed some interest were put off by the thought that nobody would take two footballers seriously enough to buy a non-football record.

Then they met Jeff Weston, a Spurs fanatic who had his own record company. He realised its potential as a pop record as opposed to another 'Nice one Cyril' or 'Tottenham, Tottenham'. Back they went into the studios and different guitars and drum beats were introduced, then there was some finalisation at Red Bus Studios (coincidentally one of the labels who turned the record down) and it was duly released.

It was the stuff of dreams, turning up at a hotel in a limousine for the launch. All the pop music press were there and many of the critics were Spurs fans who wanted to talk football while Chris and Glenn wanted to talk about music.

They appeared on Top of the Pops – this time actually knowing the words of the song – and then even guested at the London Palladium. Jimmy Tarbuck was the host. He said 'Everybody's making records – what do you think about that?' Then Chris and Glenn came on as surprise stars and Tarbuck said what a great record it was. He asked each of them a question, they were both so nervous that they quite forgot they had their own mikes and tried to talk directly into Tarbuck's. Chris got himself into the *Sunday Times* quotes of the year by saying: 'The changing room at the Palladium is no different to playing Hartlepool away.'

The record was an enormous success. It got to Number 11 in the network charts and some National Charts even showed it making the top ten. Indeed, on their way to the Palladium they had the strange experience of hearing their record played on the chart show. The most embarrassing part of it was going onto the field and having the crowd chant 'Give us a song' – at home or 'You should stick to making records' – away.

In fact the follow-up was a better record but achieved nothing despite a £20,000 video. It was a lot of fun to make but nobody ever saw it. Glenn was on his way to Monaco by then and it was hard to persuade the radio stations and record buying public to buy the record on its merits without suitable personal appearances. The pair of them even did a couple of jingles for the Simon Mayo show but doubt whether they ever saw the light of day either.

The more serious business of playing football continued and to be fair, neither Chris nor Glenn ever allowed their record career to interfere with their real professions. The Wimbledon Cup game was to be televised on the 15th March – a Sunday and on the Saturday the Spurs Squad went away to Brighton, delighted as they saw Arsenal's defeat by Watford shown on Final Score.

All week Wimbledon had been talking a good game. Spurs were soft – they had to get into them – it was their year – (they were a year too early in that respect) and Spurs had never been tackled the way they tackled. Spurs' reply was to decide that the best way to deal with it was to play football on the day. None of the First Division professionals liked playing against Wimbledon, but there is no doubt that they can be – and are – beaten by good footballing sides who play on the day.

It was all very fast and furious but Spurs always felt that at 0-0 with 20 minutes to go they would win. Ossie, Glenn, Clive and

Chris got some room and Chris got the first goal. He took the ball on his right foot, moved into the box and pulled it back onto his left foot to cross. Nigel Winterburn, then of Wimbledon now of Arsenal, stopped and with the centre-half put up his feet to stop the cross. Chris saw Dave Beasant, the Wimbledon 'keeper (who was to join Newcastle at the end of the 1987/88 season) move off the near post to anticipate the cross and so lashed the ball into the net with his right foot. After that the Dons were on the run and then, with Chris limping from one too many over enthusiastic tackles, Spurs got a free kick. Chris said to Glenn 'don't shoot'. Glenn ignored him. Chris said 'oh no' and then the ball was in the top corner of the net. Chris' injury was forgotten and he tried to jump on top of the throng of celebrating Spurs players and missed. In the bath afterwards everyone was singing, blotting out the sounds of discontent from the Wimbledon dressing room next door.

In the post-match interview, Glenn said of his free kick 'I just went up and twatted it'. Chris cringed. The word has a totally different meaning in the North-East and he couldn't believe it was being used on live television. Glenn merely said: 'My goal was for Danny'. It was typical of him to think of the injured player amidst all the celebrations.

Chris was on top of the world. The FA Cup meant far more than the Littlewoods Trophy. A home game with Liverpool beckoned that could take them nearer to the title and best of all, he just discovered that Lorna was pregnant. What could possibly stop him fulfilling all his ambitions in one season?

# CHAPTER 35

Spurs were getting used to the TV cameras, for the Liverpool game was also televised live. Spurs won 1-0 with Chris scoring a mis-hit shot that skidded and then bounced over Bruce Grobelaar. As Chris says, 'it was the power of it that beat him'. On the day however Spurs and Chris played well and as *The Mirror* reported 'Chris Waddle's brilliance and Bruce Grobelaar's blunder have set up an exciting climax to the Championship. Waddle is the winger England fans love to hate. He's frequently booed at Wembley – but now he is silencing the critics and his will be one of the first names that Bobby Robson will write into his England team for the game against Northern Ireland next month'. Spurs were 14 points behind but they did have five games in hand.

Spurs moved up to the North-East for a mid-week fixture against Newcastle and Chris took the opportunity to visit his father in hospital. There was no real change in Joe's condition and Chris found it heartbreaking to see the man who had once been so active confined to a hospital bed. Glenn scored in a 1-1 draw and with a 3-1 defeat at Luton, the title seemed to be slipping away. Chris scored but Pleat's old team really hammered his new one accompanied by the fans taunts of 'you should have stayed where you were'.

Against Norwich in the following match, the crowds showed their fickleness by aiming their abuse at Clive Allen. Then in the last ten minutes he scored a hat-trick, and became the hero, getting another match ball to add to his garage full. At 1-0 win against Sheffield Wednesday (Allen again) saw Spurs edging to the top three for the first time behind Everton and Liverpool but they knew they had to win every game to keep in touch.

The FA Cup semi-final was due to take place on the 11th April at Villa Park against Watford. The team went up to the Midlands the night before and tried to relax. It wasn't easy. On the day of the match Chris, who was rooming with Glenn by now, was up at 6.0

am and Glenn opened his eyes nearly two hours later to see his friend fully dressed sitting on an armchair reading the newspaper.

Watford had lost both their experienced goalkeepers the week before and in the team talk beforehand David Pleat said that young Plumley would be either a hero or a villain. Within 20 minutes Spurs were three up and it was mainly down to the 'keeper. At the final whistle Chris actually cried. He had got to Wembley. The fans got a bit overexcited and ran onto the pitch and Chris found himself pushed all over the place, but on the coach it was the best day ever. Champagne flowed and all three lanes of the M1 were filled with convoys of Tottenham fans. The wives were there to welcome them home, followed by a party. Once the team has actually done the hard work and got to Wembley, the rest becomes something of a dream.

The League season began to disintegrate. They drew with Manchester City, beat Charlton but lost to West Ham and could only draw with Wimbledon. They were still third but were trailing in the wake of the Merseyside giants and it looked as if they would have to settle for being London's top club – no mean achievement in itself. Chris was rested against Charlton and Wimbledon because of a suspected groin strain – which in fact was the start of a hernia problem that led to a double operation the following year. He was back to score against Oxford but when they lost 2-0 to Forest, the last mathematical chance of the title disappeared.

Glenn Hoddle's star was also disappearing over the horizon. He scored what was to be his last goal for the Club against Oxford and then by the last home game of the season against Manchester United, everybody knew he was going. Glenn is very much his own man and kept it all to himself despite his close friendship with Chris. There was little said between them on the subject but obviously Chris wished him well. Glenn had been a great servant to Tottenham but was feeling stale and it did not matter what inducement Spurs may have offered, he would not have stayed.

Chris felt sad at his departure but at the same time thought it might mean a new role for him. *The Sun* in March had already written a story headlined 'Waddle, the new Hoddle' when he had brilliantly filled Glenn's creative role against QPR. For England too his involvement was changing. He scored against Northern Ireland in a 2-0 win at the beginning of April, revelling in the freer role given to him by Bobby Robson. He tried to ignore the booing that greeted his Wembley appearance, preferring to think the abuse came from jealous Arsenal supporters and disillusioned Geordies.

# WADDLE

It wasn't pleasant though and in footballing terms he could not understand what he had done to deserve it nor what he could do to stop it. Now he was becoming a fixture in the squad although he still could never be certain of playing for a full 90 minutes.

In his personal life however there was a tragedy. Lorna had a miscarriage. The writer clearly remembers the day when Chris had received confirmation from Lorna that she was expecting a baby and he Chris, Len Lazarus and Gary Wicks went to a Kosher Chinese Restaurant and celebrated with a bottle of champagne. Now the baby was lost and as he said then and reiterates now, he would have exchanged any success in football to have saved that life. Yet he was young, they were both healthy, and the specialist said there was no reason why there should not be another chance. As ever in his life, Chris looked at the future and felt sure it would turn out alright.

The last game of the season for Spurs was against Everton and was the most controversial. Hughton and Claesen played but the rest of the team were young reserves. Everton had already won the title and the match was meaningless. As it was, the youngsters put up a good display in losing only 1-0 but the Club was fined for it. There was a feeling of injustice but Wembley lay ahead and the incident was soon forgotten.

The build-up to the Final went smoothly – too smoothly. There were the usual press conferences and Chris was photographed with Maria Whittaker which raised a few eyebrows in the Waddle household. Monday, Tuesday and Wednesday the team just trained as usual and then they were off to stay at Henloe Grange for general relaxation and health treatment. Jim Rosenthal came down to interview them and was given a wax bath for his troubles. While he was interviewing Glenn in the massage room, a mirror fell off the wall and smashed. Everybody muttered about '7 years bad luck', for footballers are the most superstitious creatures.

On the Friday they went to stay at the Pondesbourne Hotel, again unwilling to break winning precedents. In fact the hotel had changed hands and was owned and used by Tesco as a staff training centre. They agreed to let Spurs use it and Chris was back where he had stayed when he first came to London. It was only a couple of years before but it could have been a different century. If he had met that same Chris Waddle who had come down from Newcastle, it's doubtful if he would have recognised him.

The ITV cameras were on the coach on the way to the ground. Everybody thought they were going to win, confidence was high and they knew they would score whoever they played. The only worry was that there was to be a problem if Coventry pumped high balls into the box because both Regis and Houchin were good in the air. All the bookmakers who made Spurs hot favourites had forgotten the 3-2 defeat earlier in the season.

It was a great feeling going up Wembley way. Other players who had played at Wembley had told Chris they could not remember it at all clearly but Chris was determined to take the day in, to take mental photographs to keep forever in the album in his mind's eye. The team coach was surrounded by Spurs supporters and there was no sign of the opposition. He guessed they had come down from the Midlands early to make a day of it and were all in the ground.

They walked out onto the pitch because the teams are not allowed to warm up on the field. He saw Lorna in the crowd, waved to her and went back to the changing room to sit with nerves tingling, not even watching the celebrity match that went before. The sound of the band and the crowds came to them from a distance for they were all in a world of their own.

As they came out the noise was deafening. The Spurs fans were mainly at the tunnel end and totally out shouted the Coventry supporters. Although Chris just wanted to run around and kick the ball, the endless formalities had to be gone through. Nobody really wants to be introduced to a total stranger on a day like that even if they are royalty or a high placed dignitary; but the players have to accept that Cup Final Day is not just about football, just as Ascot is not only about racing, Henley about rowing nor Wimbledon concerned merely with tennis. These are days that belong to the nation.

The players peeled off their track suits and then somebody noticed only four or five of them had Holsten, the sponsor's name printed on their shorts, the rest were plain. It was only a small incident but it was a mistake. It was something that had gone wrong and it was the first cloud in a clear blue sky on what should have been a perfect day. A clear blue sky, that itself was ominous as the Coventry supporters let fly with their own sky blue song. The whistle went and the match was finally underway. Ninety minutes away from the medal he had promised himself, Lorna, and perhaps, most of all, his father.

153

# CHAPTER 36

Chris clearly had the beating of Gregg Downs at first. Glenn put in a free kick and when it came back to Chris he was going to pass it to Glenn then run forward. He saw Downs' foot rise and so he put it down the line with his right foot and went past him. Clive Allen had been told that if Chris got it on the right foot he should get into the near post. Chris crossed it in, Clive met it perfectly with his head and within 2 minutes Spurs were in front. It looked like a massacre might be on the cards.

Chris ran to the halfway line in disbelief. With hindsight a lot of people said Spurs scored too early but he feels that is rubbish. In fact the goal relaxed Tottenham and settled everybody down and Coventry's equaliser after a succession of long balls pumped in was really against the run of play. Spurs went back in front before half-time and went into the dressing room thinking the job was half over. They were wrong. Coventry to their credit kept plugging away and equalised once more to take the game into extra time where, with two tired teams, it was felt that whoever scored would win it. As it was, the winner for Coventry was an own-goal and although Chris played his heart out to the very end, it was not to be.

Everybody was drained. The fans gave them a great reception even in defeat and the Coventry supporters were particularly sporting. Their fans seemed not to know quite how to celebrate their victory so strange a bedfellow was it.

On the coach back everybody was down. Throughout their Cup adventures they had always played Beatles tapes and after 20 minutes or so of funereal silence, they put the tape on. By the time they got back to the hotel everybody was singing. It had, after all, been a great game and one, for once, where the losers would not be forgotten.

There was a reception at the ground and the applause that greeted the team was a genuine demonstration of sympathy and

154

affection. Chas and Dave were there and the other duo, Chris and Glenn killed their song as well and the party didn't finish until the early hours of the morning.

There was no time for Chris, at least, to reflect on what might have been, for on the Sunday he had to join up with the England Squad to play against Brazil the following Tuesday in the Rous Cup. England drew 1-1 against a lively young Brazilian side led up front by Mirandinha who scored the Brazilian goal. It was the first time that Chris had seen the little man who was to wear his Number 9 shirt at Newcastle and he was impressed. Mira was very sharp on the ball and although he wanted to dribble all the time in the first half, in the second 45 minutes he began to spray it around. Little was the writer to know, sitting in the stands, that within a year he would also be representing the Brazilian's interest in England. Gary Lineker scored England's goal wearing odd boots representing two different manufacturers as one of his boots had been damaged before the match. It took more than a pair of non-matching boots to curb his goal scoring talents.

A very poor goalless draw against Scotland followed and Brazil beat Scotland and took the trophy. Spurs then took their players on a Club holiday to Miami for 10 days where they played the Columbian champions, Millionaires, in a friendly and lost 1-0. In fact, Spurs did well to achieve that result for the Columbian team took the fixtures seriously and Spurs were without Clemence and Parks, Gough, Glenn, Nico and Mabbutt and played a young apprentice in goal.

The wives were again left a home. It's a difficult life to be married to a professional footballer who in turn is married to the game; but then it's a relatively short life and with an accepted retirement age of 35 for pension purposes it does not last forever. However, a manager's life is even more demanding in terms of time and it takes a very special sort of woman to see such a relationship through. Chris, in Lorna, is lucky to have found such a woman.

Miami was very hot. On the first day there Chris went out with Steve Hodge to buy some sun tan lotion. Steve decided to buy some deep tan 'frying' oil and said proudly that he never burned. Chris spent about an hour in the sun and decided enough was enough but Steve lay there all day. He came down the next day in agony, red as a lobster wearing a thick sweat shirt, long sleeves, a track suit and a towel on his head despite the heat. He turned to Mitchell Thomas and said 'Does the shower hurt *you* when you get into it?'

# WADDLE

Lorna flew out to join Chris and together they enjoyed the thrills of Disneyland before meeting up with Graham and Ann Roberts and their daughter Holly for a coaching course. They spent two weeks in Tallahasee, a week in Alabama 4 days in Tampa and Clearwater. Chris loves the States but does not know if he could live there.

Miami had been very rough and a bit frightening but Tallahasee was an industrial town with some nice areas. It had an excellent nightlife and Chris was particularly fond of one club called 'Brubaker' with a huge car in it where they used to play music from the 50's and 60's. The DJ mimed to all the records and knew all the words, however old the songs, although he was only in his mid-twenties. When they had played one particular track – 'Soul Man' all the bar staff would get up on to the counter and dance.

Clearwater on the other hand was very pretty, right on the beach with every incentive to relax. All the kids Chris and Graham saw were very keen but the majority were goalkeepers. There was no doubt in Chris' mind that there is a future for the sport in the States but they have to get to the children when they are really young. Maybe now they have got the 1994 World Cup, that will be the signal for the long delayed explosion of the sport there.

In Alabama Chris met Harold Schumacher the German keeper. He did not discuss the famous punch with him – he is a big man! The kids were predominantly black and they and everybody he met all talked with a deep southern accent that almost rubbed off a bit on both Chris and Graham.

By the time they got back to England, the new season was almost ready to start. Spurs didn't seem the same without Glenn. Johnny Metgod and Chris Fairclough had arrived and Chris had appointed Denis Roach, Glenn's agent, to develop his promotional career in the south. There was a general feeling of change in the air. Chris had a high regard for Fairclough having played up front against him for Newcastle. He is a very strong hard player with a good attitude as well as being a very likeable person. He is still only young and perhaps the best thing he has going for him is his temperament. He is very placid and never gets angry yet still manages to be the strongest tackler Chris has ever played against.

Metgod of course was famous for his dead ball kicks and vast experience both on the Continent and with Forest. He was probably brought in to replace Glenn but, in fact, as was demonstrated on the pre-season tour in Sweden, his game was

156

more like Ardiles'. Pleat still liked a five man midfield and Metgod suffered a series of injuries and never really fitted in. Many people felt that Chris should have been given the chance to replace Glenn and deep down Chris wanted it himself. Maybe Pleat would have implemented the idea later but right then he told Chris he still felt he had a lot to offer on the wing.

Chris' best position is still a conundrum and perhaps his career has suffered slightly because he can play well in so many roles. A striker for Newcastle, left- or right-wing for England, a free-roaming role and midfield for Spurs.

Even at 27 the best is yet to be seen from Chris Waddle in whatever transpires to be his best position.

# CHAPTER 37

Before Spurs left for Sweden they played the usual pre-season friendlies against the likes of Bournemouth and Exeter. Their confidence was not high and out of five games they only won two. Although they did not find scoring difficult they were letting in easy early goals. It was no great comfort to them that many people say that if a team has difficulties pre-season, they have a good year. The smashed mirror on the dressing room wall was still fresh in their minds.

As fate would have it, their first game was away to Coventry. The match was nothing like the Cup Final except as far as the result was concerned, and although Mabbutt scored, Spurs lost 2-1 without playing very well. Once again they met Newcastle early on in the the season and were 3-0 up at half-time with Chris scoring one of his best ever goals. David McCreery pulled one back in the second half but Spurs still coasted home. The fans seemed much more philosophical as far as Chris was concerned and it is to be hoped that the worst is over in that respect.

Results began to improve. They beat Chelsea and drew with an uninspiring Watford side who had the mark of a relegation team on them even then. Against Oxford Chris scored playing on the right-wing but twinges were starting across his stomach. It was a disturbing pain but not really agony and it didn't stop Chris going to Germany with England where he was injured in a 3-1 defeat.

It was his first international on German soil and going into an early tackle he slid to poke the ball away, stretched, hit his heel and jarred it. That *was* painful. It was strapped up at half-time and he had to come off. Many newspapers slaughtered him for his performance, but none bothered to enquire as to the seriousness of the injury. Chris' relationship with the Press, both tabloids and so-called heavyweights, has never been of the best. Many years ago David Miller wrote in *The Times*:

'Waddle is a winger who most of the time is reluctant to play on

158

the wing, who puzzles his colleagues as much as the opposition and around whom it is almost impossible to build a consistent pattern of play. As often as not when receiving a ball he turns inside or even back ... Waddle, though often exciting, is simultaneously exasperating and promotes a lack of teamwork which ought to be a warning to Bobby Robson, the England manager.'

In any event, on the Thursday after the match Chris walked into the Club with his foot swollen. They said it would go down with ice, but by the next day it was still not right. Over the next few weeks it became a great worry. He had never been out of the game for so long and it stretched his patience to the limits. The injury would ease off, he would start jogging and it would flare up again. It continued like that for five or six weeks, during which time he kept seeing a specialist. He then decided to take a second opinion which confirmed to him that there was considerable inflammation inside the heel and that he should take two weeks complete rest.

The Club were very supportive during what was for them a difficult period. David Pleat had left in the most bizarre of circumstances. The players had been shocked when the initial story broke of his alleged involvement with a prostitute but then as far as they were concerned it was all history while he had been with Luton and nothing to do with Spurs. However, he was unable to resist the second wave of publicity and he was gone. The players again merely learned about it from the papers. He said no goodbyes not to anybody, he just went and Trevor Hartley had a very brief spell in charge then to be replaced by Doug Livermore with Ossie Ardiles and Ray Clemence helping.

Chris was totally down and was frightened that the injury might need surgery. He was invited to go to Monaco for a rest and with the encouragement of Irving Scholar, he went off to stay with Glenn. Monaco was beautiful and he had a really good time with Glenn and Mark Hateley. As a remedy he paddled every day in the sea, a far cry from the cold of Whitley Bay where the Newcastle players had been sent for similar treatment. After a couple of days the pain went and within two days of getting back to England, he felt fit to train.

During his enforced absence he had the opportunity of spending much more time with Lorna than was usual during the season. She was pregnant again and what with her morning sickness and Chris' injury-fuelled depression, the household was none too happy. Chris lives for playing football and was simply not used to the enforced inactivity. Even for Chris Waddle there is only so much television you can watch!

Spurs had not thrived in his absence. From third place at Pleat's departure, they had tumbled below the halfway mark and although Terry Venables' appointment was welcomed by the players and supporters alike, El Tel would not be available until December. Terry, in fact, took up the reins for the Charlton match on the 13th Decenber, a game Spurs – now without Richard Gough who had not settled in London – promptly lost.

Chris had heard a lot of good things about Terry. Of the squad only Clive Allen had played under him but Chris had had a brief exposure to his methods with the Under-21 Squad and Glen Roeder, the Newcastle captain had been a great Venables fan. He made no startling changes when he arrived merely telling everyone to go out and play while trying to concentrate in practice on the back four. The Spurs ill luck continued however for heavy rain before and after Terry's arrival meant the training ground was unusable and even the first team had to train in a gym. Eventually in desperation they went to Brighton and the rain followed them there by the bucketful.

Despite the difficulties, Venables seemed to be getting it right. They beat Derby 2-1 live on television and although they lost at Southampton, they beat West Ham and Watford and drew with Chelsea to bring 1987 to a fairly hopeful close.

Drawn away to Oldham in the Cup, everybody predicted a shock, but Spurs ran out 4-2 winners. Chris scored and the whole team played really well.

However, Chris' personal disasters for the season were not over – in fact were only just beginning. After a 2-2 home draw with Coventry (who really had the Indian sign on Spurs) Chris had a dull ache in his stomach again and felt he knew himself it was a hernia. The team lost 2-0 at Newcastle, the first time his old team had beaten them since his transfer, and young Paul Gascoigne scored both. In fact Spurs hit the crossbar with a free kick and nearly grabbed a draw at the end but the inevitable headlines were 'New boy outshines old star'.

Everybody asked Chris what he thought of Paul but all he said was he should be left alone to get on with his football. Paul is very lively but there is no mischief in him at all and Chris knows he would do anything for anybody. He has to be careful that the Press don't create a false troublesome reputation that he feels he has to live up to. Now that he has joined Chris at White Hart Lane there is no doubt that the enormous respect Paul feels for Chris was one of the telling factors which helped him decide which club to sign for.

The Cup then took Spurs to the wasteland of the Potteries. Chris had never been to Port Vale before and was surprised by the size of the pitch – it was not only massive but also very heavy. The Spurs players, however, did not feel they were going to be the subject of a Cup upset. Chris had been used to it in Newcastle. Up there they had the pressure from the Press with headlines such as 'Will Newcastle fall again?' almost writing themselves. However, Spurs always thought they were too good for that sort of thing – that is until they found themselves 2-0 down to Port Vale before anything happened. Neil Ruddock pulled one back but Vale held on and Spurs, Terry Venables and all were out of the Cup.

El Tel is not a shouting sort of Manager. He'll take the players aside privately on the Monday and tell them what he thought was wrong – something much appreciated by those who play for him. Many managers will go into the dressing room and slaughter players after the final whistle saying things they can only regret afterwards. Chris understands that it must be very hard to watch a team in which you have invested so much time and effort play badly and be able to restrain yourself but for him there is no doubt it's the right way. If Chris ever goes into management, it's one of the lessons he has learnt.

After the Cup exit it wasn't just pride that was bruised because Chris was aching very badly. There was no match the next Saturday but Spurs then drew 0-0 with Oxford in what happens to be the worst game in which Chris Waddle ever took part.

Despite all his injuries, Bobby Robson still clearly saw him as a vital part of his European Championship plans and he was invited for a return trip to Israel. Clive Allen played up front and a mediocre Israeli team held a weak England side, captained by Peter Beardsley, to a goalless draw. It obviously occurred to Chris that with his experience he might have been called upon to lead the team and he only hopes that his time will come for that honour. Until he has actually done it he will never know if he is capable of it.

In Chris' experience it's not just the Captain of the team who can be the most inspirational. Although Richard Gough was Spurs' Captain, there is no doubt that Glenn or Ray Clemence had more influence on the field and last season's youngsters such as Paul Moran and Brian Statham turned to Chris for advice. In his early days at Newcastle Chris complained to Jeff Clarke that Arthur Cox always seemed to be picking on him. Clarke said 'wait until you have had a few more managers – you'll say how good Coxie was'. The words were prophetic.

After the England match in which Mick Harford made his long awaited debut, Chris saw the England doctor who confirmed his self-diagnosis of a hernia. On his return to England he asked John Sheridan the Spurs physiotherapist to make arrangements for a check-up. He undressed and lay on the bed while the doctor explored the 'canal' and asked him to cough. He almost hit the ceiling with the pain and when the doctor told him it was a double hernia he knew he was in for yet another period out of the game.

It seems incredible that in all his time in the profession he had never had a serious injury before the 87/88 season yet here were two such misfortunes in a short period of time. The doctor told him they wanted him to come in as soon as possible. Chris looked up pleadingly knowing there was a First Division fixture against Manchester United the next day. 'Can I play?' he asked. The doctor nodded. He and Chris both knew it would be his last game for some considerable time.

# CHAPTER 38

It says a lot for Chris Waddle's determination that he was prepared to go out and compete in pain. Too many people think he is a soft touch, that the slouched shoulders and permanent look of exhaustion mean he is not prepared to compete. They could not be more wrong for he is one of the most competitive and indeed physically fit players in the League.

Paul Walsh signed from Liverpool and was making his debut and looked good in a 1-1 draw. Chris had always rated him as a player, very tidy, very tricky, good in the air and with the strength and ability to hold the ball up. He also had the rare talent of being able to run into the corner of the box which always helps a winger get the ball into him. Nottingham Forest operated that system most successfully with Roberts and Birtles and Woodcock. The defender is also made nervous because he knows a mistimed tackle can lead to a penalty.

On the 24th February, the following day, Chris entered the Princess Grace Clinic for the operation. He was given a pre-med which was supposed to make him relaxed but which had little effect at all. He lay there dejectedly watching television and thinking of the Tottenham training session he was missing. Eventually two men wheeled him away. He waited in a queue outside the theatre. It was a busy day for hernia operations!

He knew nothing else until he was woken up at 6.00 or 7.00 at night, in agony.

It was very sore the next day as well and he had to have pain killing tablets yet at 8.00 in the morning, the Sisters of Mercy appeared and told him to get up because they had to make his bed.

'No way,' said Chris but they prevailed and sent him off to wash. He couldn't straighten up and stumbled to the bathroom bent right over, or as someone cruelly suggested, walking normally for him.

He became friendly with Martin Hinkard from Altrincham who

163

was in for the same operation. Although it hurt, they still managed some good laughs until after a few days of boredom and confinement they felt they were in the cast of *One flew over the cuckoos nest* – it was time to escape. They went out to Madame Tussauds' determined not to laugh but laughing even more because of that determination. It took them 10 minutes to walk the 60 or 70 yards and when they got out of the lift they were faced with an effigy of Benny Hill. Both of them collapsed with laughter and tears of pain and it took them a quarter of an hour just to get in. They were soon so exhausted they had to return to get more painkillers.

The next day Spurs beat Sheffield Wednesday 3-1 away. Steve Hodge, Gary Mabbutt, Mitchell Thomas had all been in to visit but Chris and Martin decided to go to the pub to celebrate still wearing slippers and hospital armbands.

Martin went into such paroxysms of laughter that he had to return to get painkillers but Chris stayed to finish his drink. The door opened and there was one Terence Venables saying 'I thought I would find you here.' They had a couple of drinks and a good chat. Many managers would have exploded but Terry had been a player and understands players. Together with Alan Harris they make a wonderful partnership and certainly amongst professionals he is regarded as the most approachable of men and the most understanding.

Discharged from hospital, Chris returned home to make Lorna's life a misery – although it was still not as bad as the foot injury. At least he knew it was over and in six weeks he would be back playing. For three weeks he did nothing then started walking and jogging finally returning to play in a reserve match against Fulham. Another reserve match and it was back to first team duty when he came on as a substitute against QPR with Spurs 1-0 down. They were 2-0 down before he touched the ball. Liverpool away were a daunting task in the 87/88 season. Spurs played well lost 1-0 and Liverpool duly pocketed the Championship.

While Chris had been away Spurs had been sliding towards the play off zone and many supporters were cynically looking forward to the play offs to give their season some meaning. However a 1-1 draw with Charlton saw Spurs mathematically safe. What was for them, as a team, and Chris in particular, a disastrous season ended with a 2-1 win over Luton.

Meanwhile Chris had been duly recalled to the England Squad for the Rous Cup. They beat Scotland 1-0 with Chris replacing

Trevor Steven and he then started the game against the exciting and dazzling Columbians, and it was his cross that made Lineker's goal. He felt he had had a good game, his passing was good and he was taking men on. He was still taking them on when he was substituted, perhaps because Bobby Robson still doubted his full fitness.

After England duly won the Cup it was off to Lausanne in Switzerland for the last friendly before the European Championships. Lausanne was beautiful, very much like Monaco and very expensive. Chris came on in the second-half of a goalless draw and did not impress. The Swiss, like so many other European nations, played a sweeper system which messes up a winger's game more than most. Chris' strength is on the ball, not off it. If it were a League match in England the manager would move him around but playing for his country against the sweeper system means that as a winger he can't get at the full-back who always has cover. It's not an excuse, its a fact, and perhaps, if England are able to achieve anything again in our lifetime, they have to come into step with the rest of Europe.

After the Swiss game, Robson named his squad for Germany and, despite doubts expressed in one or two papers, confirmed that Chris was on the plane. He had won his battle for fitness, triumphed over a season of total adversity. His selection and one other little matter made him forget all that had gone before. He became a father.

Lorna had wanted him to be there but the odds were that the baby would be born during the Championships. It was decided that if the birth had not occurred by the 30th May, that it would be induced and that was what happened. Finally it was a caesarian birth and Chris *was* there. The delivery took but 10 minutes and the doctor turned to Chris and confirmed it was a girl, something they had both known since the scan a few months earlier. Chris lifted her up in shock thinking: 'How the hell did something that size come out of there'. It was the best moment of his life and all the cups and internationals, all the goals and glory faded into total insignificance.

Although they had a while to choose a name, it was still not decided. It was down to Brooke or Jade but as Jade had been in the news so much because of Mick Jagger's daughter they stettled on Brooke. As Chris says, if they have a boy next they can call him Bond. There was no second name. Chris' parents had seen to that by christening their sons Joseph Wayne, Richard Wilfred and

# WADDLE

Christoper Roland. Chris kissed Lorna and the baby, told his sleepy daughter he would like to bring a medal back for her and set off to join the England Squad.

# CHAPTER 39

The Squad assembled at High Wycombe and Chris and the rest of them received their England blazers and went to celebrate the 125th Anniversary of the FA. The next day they played Aylesbury before 6,000 crowd and won 7-0. Chris had to come off after an hour with a knock on the top of his thigh and although he could kick the ball the thought 'oh no, not again, not another injury' still crossed his mind. Trevor Steven and Mark Hateley also picked up injuries and Gary Lineker had a sore toe. Monday and Tuesday meant treatment for the walking wounded, light training for the rest of the Squad and then it was off to Germany from Luton.

To keep them match sharp Bobby Robson had arranged another friendly against a German non-league team. Of course with hindsight everybody can be clever, but the match turned out to be not so friendly as Lineker, Wright and Steven were all injured and even Gary Steven, usually the fittest of players, picked up a knock.

By the time of the first match against Jack Charlton's Republic of Ireland everybody looked very tired. Trevor Steven was not fit and Chris started the match. England had loads of chances but Eire scored with their one. The Irish lads chased everything and were clearly the fresher, fitter team. All they had done in the build up was to play five-a-side and work on set pieces.

Jackie Charlton was very friendly. Chris had only fallen out with them over the contract and had always been able to talk to him on a one-to-one basis. Off the pitch it was never difficult going. Jack shook hands with Chris before the match and Chris wished him luck afterwards. The pair of them finally healing a rift that had lasted for three years.

Chris had always felt an international job would suit Jack better than a club appointment. He told the story on television of Jack taking the training at Newcastle and being interrupted by a fast car roaring into the Training Ground with the driver shouting 'trout on the Tweed.' Jack said to Willie McFaul 'take the training. I'll see you in a couple of days.'

Jack liked shooting and fishing and the facility in international terms not to have to see your players every day lets him live his life to the full. He had obviously done well with the limited resources available to him. The Republic players like him and it was, without doubt, the happiest squad of the Championships.

The English fans were disappointing compared to the Irish supporters. All Chris will say to point up the difference between the two sets is that the Irish fans sang along with *With Or Without You* on the loudspeaker and the English supporters refused to join in the Mexican wave and instead gave 'V' signs.

The English Squad saw no trouble themselves and indeed the writer and Len Lazarus who went out for the Holland game both felt that the reports of the death of English football had been greatly exaggerated. Colin Moynihan, our 'Minister of Sport', had been talking British Clubs out of Europe since the start of the season and unable to tell the real troublemakers' nationality, he returned from Germany no wiser about our national sport. There was no doubt there were some English hooligans there out for trouble and equally no doubt the drink got the better of others, but the attitude of the politicians and the newspapers was nothing short of disgraceful. The English and Dutch fans walked together, talked together and drank together. Perhaps Mr Moynihan should stick to rowing and rugby which he doubtless understands and leave our national game to those who appreciate it. Unless and until English Clubs get back into Europe – and there can be no argument against allowing the likes of Everton to play – they will never be successful at international level. We need to play against the top European Clubs to take on European countries.

Even after the Irish game though, the English team were not really down. They felt they had been unlucky but they could still do it. They moved onto the splendid Guthohne Hotel near Dusseldorf and were greatly entertained by Kenny Sansom, Chris' room mate for the trip, who did incredible impressions of Prince Charles, Norman Wisdom, Ronald Regan, Harold Steptoe and Cary Grant. Chris is convinced that he has a great future on the stage when he leaves football.

Bobby Robson decided on a more defensive formation against the Dutch. He didn't tell Chris directly that he had been relegated to substitute, he merely announced the team. Chris was disappointed that he would not start the match, but the important thing was that the team should beat Holland.

A hot day in Dusseldorf and the Stadium filled with some 30,000 Dutch supporters compared to 9,000 or 10,000 English fans. The police were out in force but in the Stadium the English horde was perfectly behaved giving their team wonderful support even when they fell behind most unluckily just before half-time. In the second-half they fought back magnificently and after Bryan Robson equalised, Holland were on the ropes for 20 minutes. The stadium echoed to the English voices and then Trevor Steven picked up a knee injury and Chris was sent on. Before he could even kick the ball England were 3-1 down and Mark Hateley came on in a last desperate throw of the dice. In Mexico Waddle and Hateley had been dropped before the Poland victory, now they were on to try and rescue England; but the game had gone beyond recall.

There was little consolation in thinking that if Ireland beat Russia and England did the same with Ireland holding Holland, there was still a chance. All the way back from the Stadium in a tram the supporters were doing their calculations until some wit shouted out 'We'll be the only team to qualify without a point!' The players sat down to dinner in the Hotel and momentarily brightened up at Whelan's brilliant goal but the Irish needed to play 90 minutes at breakneck speed and as Russia equalised against the tired Republic side, England were out.

Against Russia, a match aimed at restoring England's pride, Chris was not even a substitute. Again Bobby Robson gave no explanation but with the way the Russians took England apart, Chris was better off out of it. The Russians were a great team at making runs with perfect timing but England played really badly, even the men who played regularly in Europe being unable to produce anything special on this occasion.

He was really pleased to be going home. He had played for only 110 minutes although poor Viv Anderson had attended yet another major tournament without having a kick. It's hard to believe he could have done worse than some who did play. The same applies to Peter Reid who, grateful for the holiday, must surely have lent his aggression to a midfield that was at times virtually non-existent. Chris refuses to criticise the manager. He is the man in charge, he picks the team on the day and if it works he is the Messiah, if it fails he takes the responsibility.

Everybody landed at Heathrow. He collected his bags and walked to the terminal with Glenn. Glenn's wife was there but she hadn't seen Lorna. Chris then received a call at the Information Desk. It was Lorna on the phone. She was at Luton! It was the perfect end to a perfect tour. He got into a cab and arrived home just as she turned into the drive. Brooke was waiting for him just as she will now always be waiting. Joe Senior was told of her birth and even gravely ill in hospital, became very animated and excited. The life cycle continues. The Waddles are a family. No more lonely Christmases with just the two of them. There is a shape, a dimension beyond football.

Yet their life is still inextricably linked with the game. The fixture list will have to be studied to fix a date for the christening with Spurs away to Newcastle and Liverpool. The 88/89 season beckons. Despite all rumours, Chris still has 2 years left on his contract with Tottenham Hotspur and will give all he has got. He is looking for a year without injury, a year of success and challenge, a year in which his career and his daughter can both blossom.

It's all a long way from the dole queue and the academic failure, from the rejection by so many clubs. It's a far cry from fish and chips, from Leam Lane, from Tow Law. Chris Waddle has come an awfully long way, yet one has the feeling he has a long way still to go.

# Chris Waddle – Career Statistics

## Compiled by Andy Porter

*Football League History*

Chris made his Football League debut on October 22 1980 when Shrewsbury Town visited St James' Park for a Second Division fixture. Newcastle won 1-0 thanks to a second-half goal by Bobby Shinton. Their full line-up that Wednesday evening was; Carr, Carney, Withe, Martin, Boam, Mitchell, Shinton, Wharton, Waddle, Rafferty, Hibbitt.

On his ninth league appearance Chris netted his first League goal. Terry Venables' QPR were the visitors on February 7 1981, Chris' second-half goal being the only one of the game.

Chris played his final match for Newcastle at Norwich City on May 11 1985 and his last in front of a home crowd five days earlier, when Tottenham won 3-2. In his first League season at Newcastle he was partnered up front on two occasions by former Spur Ray Clarke, in his last home game against Tottenham, his new Spurs team mate Paul Gascoigne came on as substitute for Newcastle.

August 17 1985 saw Chris score twice on his League debut for Spurs. Watford were the opponents at White Hart Lane on the opening day of a new season which saw the visitors beaten 4-0. Both Chris' goals were headers, the first coming on 22 minutes from a cross by fellow debutant Paul Allen, the second afrter 68 minutes, following a centre by Tony Galvin. Spurs' team that afternoon was; Clemence, Thomas, Hughton, Allen (P), Miller, Perryman (sub. Leworthy), Ardiles, Falco, Waddle, Hazard, Galvin.

Between October 23 1982 and December 29 1984 Chris made 96 consecutive League appearances in his best run of League football. Altogether he has scored 65 goals in the League, made up of 50 single-goal strikes, six two-goal matches and one hat-trick. This latter was at Loftus Road on September 22 1984 in the space of 27 minutes.From 4-0 up at half-time Newcastle hung on to gain a point from a 5-5 draw with QPR.

December 1983 saw Chris score in five consecutive League games, notching six goals, to create his best run of goalscoring in League football.

171

# League Appearances and Goals by Club by Season

| CLUB | TOTAL APP | TOTAL GLS | 1980-81 APP | 1980-81 GLS | 1981-82 APP | 1981-82 GLS | 1982-83 APP | 1982-83 GLS | 1983-84 APP | 1983-84 GLS | 1984-85 APP | 1984-85 GLS | 1985-86 APP | 1985-86 GLS | 1986-87 APP | 1986-87 GLS | 1987-88 APP | 1987-88 GLS |
|---|---|---|---|---|---|---|---|---|---|---|---|---|---|---|---|---|---|---|
| Arsenal | 7 | | | | | | | | | | 2 | | 2 | | 2 | | 1 | |
| Aston Villa | 6 | 2 | | | | | | | | | 2 | 2 | 2 | | 2 | | | |
| Barnsley | 5 | 2 | | | 2 | | 1 | | 2 | 2 | | | | | | | | |
| Birmingham City | 1 | 1 | | | | | | | | | | | 1 | 1 | | | | |
| Blackburn Rovers | 6 | 2 | | | 2 | | 2 | 1 | 2 | 1 | | | | | | | | |
| Bolton Wanderers | 5 | 1 | 1 | | 2 | | 2 | 1 | | | | | | | | | | |
| Bright & Hove Albion | 2 | 2 | | | | | | | 2 | 2 | | | | | | | | |
| Bristol City | 1 | 1 | | | | | | | | | | | | | | | | |
| Bristol Rovers | 1 | 1 | | | | | | | | | | | | | | | | |
| Burnley | 2 | 1 | | | | | | | 2 | 1 | | | | | | | | |
| Cambridge United | 6 | | | | 2 | | 2 | | 2 | | | | | | | | | |
| Cardiff City | 5 | 1 | 1 | | 2 | | | | 2 | 1 | | | | | | | | |
| Carlisle United | 4 | 2 | | | | | 2 | | 2 | 2 | | | | | | | | |
| Charlton Athletic | 9 | 2 | | | 2 | 1 | 2 | | 2 | 1 | | | | | 1 | | 2 | |
| Chelsea | 14 | 3 | 1 | | 2 | 2 | 2 | | 2 | | 1 | 1 | 2 | | 2 | | 2 | |
| Coventry City | 7 | | | | | | | | | | 1 | | 2 | | 2 | | 2 | |
| Crystal Palace | 6 | 4 | | | 2 | 1 | 2 | 2 | 2 | 1 | | | | | | | | |
| Derby County | 8 | 4 | 1 | | 2 | 1 | 2 | 1 | 2 | 2 | | | | | | | 1 | |
| Everton | 6 | | | | | | | | | | 2 | | 2 | | 1 | | 1 | |
| Fulham | 3 | | | | | | 1 | | 2 | | | | | | | | | |
| Grimsby Town | 7 | 1 | 1 | | 2 | | 2 | | 2 | | | | | | | | | |
| Huddersfield Town | 2 | 2 | | | | | | | 2 | 2 | | | | | | | | |
| Ipswich Town | 4 | 1 | | | | | | | | | 2 | 1 | 2 | | | | | |
| Leeds United | 4 | 1 | | | | | 2 | 1 | 2 | | | | | | | | | |
| Leicester City | 10 | 1 | | | 2 | | 2 | | | | 2 | 1 | 2 | | 2 | | | |
| Liverpool | 8 | 2 | | | | | | | | | 2 | | 2 | 1 | 2 | 1 | 2 | |
| Luton Town | 10 | 1 | 1 | | 2 | | | | | | 2 | | 2 | | 2 | 1 | 1 | |
| Manchester City | 6 | 1 | | | | | | | 2 | 1 | | | 2 | | 2 | | | |
| Manchester United | 6 | | | | | | | | | | 2 | | 1 | | 2 | | 1 | |
| Middlesbrough | 4 | | | | | | 2 | | 2 | | | | | | | | | |
| Newcastle United | 6 | 2 | | | | | | | | | | | 2 | 1 | 2 | | 2 | 1 |
| Norwich City | 6 | 2 | | | 2 | 1 | | | | | 2 | 1 | | | 2 | | | |
| Nottingham Forest | 6 | | | | | | | | | | 2 | | 2 | | 2 | | | |
| Oldham Athletic | 6 | 1 | 1 | | 2 | | 1 | | 2 | 1 | | | | | | | | |
| Orient | 2 | | | | 2 | | | | | | | | | | | | | |
| Oxford United | 6 | 4 | | | | | | | | | | | 2 | 1 | 2 | 3 | 2 | |
| Portsmouth | 2 | 2 | | | | | | | 2 | 2 | | | | | | | | |
| Queens Park Rangers | 11 | 4 | 1 | 1 | 2 | | 2 | | | | 1 | 3 | 2 | | 2 | | 1 | |
| Rotherham United | 3 | | | | 2 | | 1 | | | | | | | | | | | |
| Sheffield Wednesday | 12 | 3 | | | 2 | | 2 | | 2 | | 2 | 1 | 2 | 2 | 2 | | | |
| Shrewsbury Town | 6 | | 1 | | 2 | | 1 | | 2 | | | | | | | | | |
| Southampton | 7 | 1 | | | | | | | | | 2 | | 2 | 1 | 2 | | 1 | |
| Stoke City | 2 | 1 | | | | | | | | | 2 | 1 | | | | | | |
| Swansea City | 2 | | | | | | | | 2 | | | | | | | | | |
| Tottenham Hotspur | 2 | 1 | | | | | | | | | 2 | 1 | | | | | | |
| Watford | 9 | 2 | | | 2 | | | | | | 2 | | 1 | 2 | 2 | | 2 | |
| West Bromwich Albion | 3 | 2 | | | | | | | | | 1 | | 2 | 2 | | | | |
| West Ham United | 8 | 3 | 1 | | | | | | | | 2 | | 2 | 1 | 2 | 1 | 1 | 1 |
| Wimbledon | 1 | | | | | | | | | | | | 1 | | | | | |
| Wolverhampton Wanderers | 2 | | | | | | 2 | | | | | | | | | | | |
| Wrexham | 3 | 1 | 1 | | 2 | 1 | | | | | | | | | | | | |

## International Career

Chris' international career started at The Dell, Southampton, on October 16 1984 when he played for England Under-21 at the age of 23 years and 10 months! He made a perfect start, scoring England's first goal after two minutes in the 2-0 win over Finland which opened their defence of the European Under-21 Championship.

February 1985 saw him break into the Full England Squad for a World Cup Qualifier with Northern Ireland, but he had to wait until the friendly against The Republic of Ireland the following month to make his debut for the team. Since then he has amassed 36 Caps, scoring four goals, details of which follow.

At representative level Chris had been selected once for the Football League. That was in their Centenary match against the Rest of the World at Wembley on August 8 1987, which the Football League won 3-0.

## Summary of International Appearances

| Date | Competition | Opposition | Result | Comments |
|------|-------------|-----------|--------|----------|
| 26.3.85 | Friendly | Rep of Ireland | 2-1 | |
| 1.5.85 | World Cup Qualifier | Rumania | 0-0 | sub |
| 22.5.85 | World Cup Qualifier | Finland | 1-1 | sub |
| 25.5.85 | Rous Cup | Scotland | 0-1 | sub |
| 6.6.85 | Friendly | Italy | 1-2 | replaced |
| 9.6.85 | Friendly | Mexico | 0-1 | sub |
| 12.6.85 | Friendly | West Germany | 3-0 | |
| 16.6.85 | Friendly | USA | 5-0 | replaced |
| 11.9.85 | World Cup Qualifier | Rumania | 1-1 | replaced |
| 16.10.85 | World Cup Qualifier | Turkey | 5-0 | scored one |
| 13.11.85 | World Cup Qualifier | Northern Ireland | 0-0 | |
| 26.2.86 | Friendly | Israel | 2-1 | replaced |
| 26.3.86 | Friendly | Soviet Union | 1-0 | scored one replaced |
| 23.4.86 | Rous Cup | Scotland | 2-1 | |
| 17.5.86 | Friendly | Mexico | 3-0 | replaced |
| 24.5.86 | Friendly | Canada | 1-0 | replaced |
| 3.6.86 | World Cup Finals | Portugal | 0-1 | replaced |
| 6.6.86 | World Cup Finals | Morocco | 0-0 | |
| 11.6.86 | World Cup Finals | Poland | 3-0 | sub |
| 22.6.86 | World Cup Finals | Argentina | 1-2 | sub |
| 9.9.86 | Friendly | Sweden | 0-1 | sub |
| 15.10.86 | Euro Cup Qualifier | Northern Ireland | 3-0 | scored one |
| 12.11.86 | Euro Cup Qualifier | Yugoslavia | 2-0 | replaced |
| 10.2.87 | Euro Cup Qualifier | Spain | 4-2 | replaced |
| 1.4.87 | Euro Cup Qualifier | Northern Ireland | 2-0 | scored one |
| 19.5.87 | Euro Cup Qualifier | Turkey | 0-0 | |
| 19.5.87 | Rous Cup | Brazil | 1-1 | |
| 23.5.87 | Rous Cup | Scotland | 0-0 | |
| 9.9.87 | Friendly | West Germany | 1-3 | replaced |
| 17.2.88 | Friendly | Israel | 0-0 | |
| 27.4.88 | Friendly | Hungary | 0-0 | replaced |
| 21.5.88 | Rous Cup | Scotland | 1-0 | sub |
| 24.5.88 | Rous Cup | Columbia | 1-1 | replaced |
| 28.5.88 | Friendly | Switzerland | 1-0 | sub |
| 12.6.88 | European Cup Finals | Rep of Ireland | 0-1 | |
| 15.6.88 | European Cup Finals | Netherlands | 1-3 | sub |

## Summary of Club Appearances

| Season | Football League App | Gls | FA Cup App | Gls | League Cup App | Gls | Super Cup App | Gls | Total App | Gls |
|---|---|---|---|---|---|---|---|---|---|---|
| 1980-81 | 13 | 1 | 4 | 2 | | | | | 17 | 3 |
| 1981-82 | 42 | 7 | 3 | 1 | 2 | | | | 47 | 8 |
| 1982-83 | 37 | 7 | 2 | | 1 | | | | 40 | 7 |
| 1983-84 | 42 | 18 | 1 | | 1 | | | | 44 | 18 |
| 1984-85 | 36* | 13 | 2 | 1 | 4 | 2 | | | 42 | 16 |
| NEWCASTLE | 170 | 46 | 12 | 4 | 8 | 2 | | | 190 | 52 |
| 1985-86 | 39 | 11 | 5 | 2 | 6 | 1 | 4 | | 54 | 14 |
| 1986-87 | 39 | 6 | 6 | 2 | 9 | 3 | | | 54 | 11 |
| 1987-88 | 22* | 2 | 2 | 1 | 1 | | | | 25 | 3 |
| TOTTENHAM | 100 | 19 | 13 | 5 | 16 | 4 | 4 | | 133 | 28 |
| SUM TOTAL | 270 | 65 | 25 | 9 | 24 | 6 | 4 | | 323 | 80 |

\* includes one appearance as a substitute   APP = appearances   GLS = goals

## FA Cup

Chris made an impressive FA Cup debut for Newcastle United on January 3 1981. He scored both goals in a 2-1 home win over Sheffield Wednesday which eased them into the Fourth Round.

Since then he has played in each of the two dozen matches his club has been involved in, eleven for Newcastle and thirteen since joining Tottenham. His nine goals in this competition have come in eight games, the only brace being on his debut.

| CLUB | TOTAL APP | TOTAL GLS | 1980-81 APP | GLS | 1981-82 APP | GLS | 1982-83 APP | GLS | 1983-84 APP | GLS | 1984-85 APP | GLS | 1985-86 APP | GLS | 1986-87 APP | GLS | 1987-88 APP | GLS |
|---|---|---|---|---|---|---|---|---|---|---|---|---|---|---|---|---|---|---|
| Brighton & Hove Albion | 2 | | | | | | 2 | | | | | | | | | | | |
| Colchester United | 2 | 1 | | | 2 | 1 | | | | | | | | | | | | |
| Coventry City | 1 | | | | | | | | | | | | | | 1 | | | |
| Crystal Palace | 1 | | | | | | | | | | | | | | 1 | | | |
| Everton | 1 | | | | | | | | | | | | 1 | | | | | |
| Exeter City | 2 | | 2 | | | | | | | | | | | | | | | |
| Grimsby Town | 1 | | | | | | 1 | | | | | | | | | | | |
| Liverpool | 1 | | | | | | | | 1 | | | | | | | | | |
| Luton Town | 1 | | 1 | | | | | | | | | | | | | | | |
| Newcastle United | 1 | | | | | | | | | | | | | | 1 | | | |
| Nottingham Forest | 2 | 1 | | | | | | | | | 2 | 1 | | | | | | |
| Notts County | 2 | 1 | | | | | | | | | | | 2 | 1 | | | | |
| Oldham Athletic | 1 | 1 | | | | | | | | | | | | | | | 1 | 1 |
| Oxford United | 2 | 1 | | | | | | | | | | | 2 | 1 | | | | |
| Port Vale | 1 | | | | | | | | | | | | | | 1 | | | |
| Scunthorpe United | 1 | 1 | | | | | | | | | | | | | 1 | 1 | | |
| Sheffield Wednesday | 1 | 2 | 1 | 2 | | | | | | | | | | | | | | |
| Watford | 1 | | | | | | | | | | | | | | 1 | | | |
| Wimbledon | 1 | 1 | | | | | | | | | | | | | 1 | 1 | | |

## Football League Cup
### (incorporating the Milk and Littlewoods Cups)

Fulham were the visitors to St James' Park when Chris made his League Cup debut on October 7 1981. The London club snatched a 2-1 win in the Second Round First-Leg match. Chris had to wait until his fifth appearance to taste victory in the League Cup, when Newcastle beat Bradford City 3-1 on September 26 1984. A fortnight later he scored the only goal of the Second-Leg at Bradford, securing Newcastle a Third Round place for the first time in eight years.

Chris played in twenty consecutive matches between September 26 1984 and September 23 1987 – his best run in this competition – four for Newcastle and sixteen for Tottenham. He has yet to score more than a single goal in a League Cup Match.

| CLUB | TOTAL APP | TOTAL GLS | 1981-82 APP | 1981-82 GLS | 1982-83 APP | 1982-83 GLS | 1983-84 APP | 1983-84 GLS | 1984-85 APP | 1984-85 GLS | 1985-86 APP | 1985-86 GLS | 1986-87 APP | 1986-87 GLS | 1987-88 APP | 1987-88 GLS |
|---|---|---|---|---|---|---|---|---|---|---|---|---|---|---|---|---|
| Arsenal | 3 | | | | | | | | | | | | 3 | | | |
| Barnsley | 2 | 1 | | | | | | | | | | | 2 | 1 | | |
| Birmingham City | 1 | 1 | | | | | | | | | | | 1 | 1 | | |
| Bradford City | 2 | 1 | | | | | | | 2 | 1 | | | | | | |
| Cambridge United | 1 | 1 | | | | | | | | | | | 1 | 1 | | |
| Fulham | 2 | | 2 | | | | | | | | | | | | | |
| Ipswich Town | 2 | 1 | | | | | | | 2 | 1 | | | | | | |
| Leeds United | 1 | | | | 1 | | | | | | | | | | | |
| Orient | 2 | 1 | | | | | | | | | 2 | 1 | | | | |
| Oxford United | 1 | | | | | | 1 | | | | | | | | | |
| Portsmouth | 3 | | | | | | | | | | 3 | | | | | |
| Torquay United | 1 | | | | | | | | | | | | | | | 1 |
| West Ham United | 2 | | | | | | | | | | | | 2 | | | |
| Wimbledon | 1 | | | | | | | | | | | 1 | | | | |